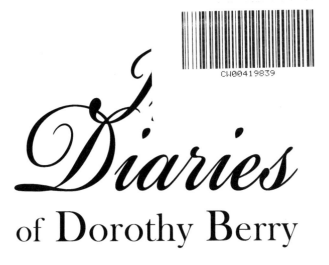

Diaries

of Dorothy Berry

A life of unwavering faith

India Diaries
of Dorothy Berry

A life of unwavering faith

compiled by

TRISHA BERRY

BROWN
DOG
BOOKS

Published under licence by Brown Dog Books and
The Self-Publishing Partnership, 7 Green Park Station, Bath BA1 1JB

www.selfpublishingpartnership.co.uk

ISBN printed book: 978-1-78545-331-1
ISBN e-book: 978-1-78545-332-8

Cover design by Kevin Rylands
Internal design by Andrew Easton

Printed and bound in the UK

INTRODUCTION

Dorothy Ada Notley left the UK aged 23, on a steamship to sail to India to be a missionary, in January 1948, five months after Indian Independence and Partition from Britain.

Undaunted by this she embraced the country, the Hindi language and the people at a time when many British were leaving!

Her detailed diaries record her extraordinary life there until 1959, along with many more trips and adventures there later in her life. She had wanted to return to Shillong for her 90th birthday but sadly a stroke, dementia and a new hip at the age of 90 made this impossible for her.

This book shows her love, her fascination and her frustrations with this vast South Asian country, and more importantly her unwavering faith shines through it all.

This book is dedicated to memories of Eddy, Dorothy and Richard Berry, from their family whose lives they filled with love, adventure and happiness.

2017

She lay peacefully in bed, her mouth tightly closed with a hint of a smile on her face.

She had been like this for a week, determined to refuse food, water and the antibiotics prescribed for a chest infection. We covered her with her beautiful Tibetan blanket.

A few days earlier she had lucidly told us:

"I am with the people up there, it's a long way up and very beautiful, everyone is with me. They want us to say thankyou to everybody and each other, wouldn't that be nice?"

She knew she was going to Heaven.

She knew she was able to make that decision.

She knew she was refusing drugs and was in control, even though dementia had taken over her incredibly intelligent and articulate mind.

We all thought she was indestructible and for most of her life she was, always on the move travelling by ships, trains, cars, bicycles, trucks, hitch-hiking and walking – all over the world.

Being so organised she had a DNR in place so doctors decided not to admit her to hospital and a morphine patch was placed on her back. The family spent the next few days beside her bed holding her hand and reminiscing with her as she peacefully drifted to sleep, knowing it was her decision. Her ashes were taken to

Bombay (now Mumbai) and placed in the warm, brown waters of the Arabian Sea at the Gate of India. Back in the land she had made her home for eleven years, the final chapter of her life, free at last.

Dorothy was born in 1925 to Stanley and Elizabeth Notley who ran a newsagent shop in Mill Hill, London. Her sister was ten years older and not particularly pleased having to babysit. Diaries were kept of her extraordinary life which are copied in the story in her own words, mostly!!

1939-1947

I was 13 and my father had four shops now and bought a house on Canford Cliffs in Dorset. When the war began my school in London was evacuated, and because my mother thought I would misbehave it was agreed I would live with her in Dorset. I joined a Crusader class on Sundays and decided after reading the Bible properly either that what Jesus said was true or that He was mad. The first idea seemed more reasonable to me so I became a Christian and knew that life went on for ever, God loved me and I was following the one who was the Way, the Truth and the Life. So my teen years in the war were good for me. I went to a local school and learnt to ride a bike which I continued to do until I was 80 when it was taken away from me when my knees stopped me pedalling...

There are many memories of cycle rides around Dorset on traffic-free roads as petrol was rationed, air-raid warnings, sitting in shelters endlessly trying to do schoolwork, or just singing songs to keep cheerful. I remember nights we were dive-bombed as German

flares drifted over us from an ammunition dump. I remember being very angry when France capitulated but never for a moment thought we would lose the war. For me the garden became an African jungle adventure, a seacoast, an expedition up a mountain or whatever took my fancy. It was always safe to go out alone and walk for miles by myself.

I passed my exams and in 1944 I won a place at Newnham College at the University of Cambridge to study mathematics, but it was way too hard, and so after scraping through my first year I swapped to Geography for which I got my BA Hons degree.

Many friendships here lasted 60 years or more, especially in the CWICCU – Cambridge Women's Inter-Collegiate Christian Union. These three years were so far the best of my life as we learnt to think for ourselves, man the fire-fighting teams, sleep outdoors in the summer and helped to map the Fenlands in freezing winters. Summers were spent helping with the harvests and punting on the River Cam, with BOYS who we were not allowed to mix with at university. The boys were, however, useful for exchanging food coupons for clothing coupons so we could buy stockings!! I had two boyfriends here both called Bob, but the relationships fizzled out as I had serious plans to travel. Sadly women were not allowed to be presented with their degrees at this point, in fact it was the following year, in 1948, that women were first allowed a degree ceremony

CWICCU 1946

Graduation 1998

actually on campus. So it was not until July 1998 that 900 women (who had all graduated separately from the men, so as not to intimidate them – at that time we were outnumbered five to one, it was rather splendid) were all invited back to Cambridge and given a proper degree ceremony with caps and gowns. I had cycled there and was interviewed on national TV.

I wanted to be a missionary and chose a place in India that helped destitute Anglo-Indian children, started by a Scottish missionary Dr Graham who had found many children abandoned in the tea plantations, railway junctions and cities of the subcontinent, whom no one wanted. From 1889 onwards Dr Graham transformed a struggling Indian mission station into a thriving community and created in Kalimpong, one of the most beautiful places in the world, a safe haven for unwanted children of mixed-blood parents.

The children were cared for in cottages surrounding the school in the foothills of the Himalayas, by European "aunties" and European sponsors. My parents thought I was quite mad given the recent unrest in India following Partition and Independence in August 1947. No one could have predicted the horror that lay ahead after Partition. The great Mahatma Gandhi from his ashram in Calcutta said, "I have no message to give Independence because my heart has dried up." The British were leaving in droves and I had chosen to go there.

1948

This year saw another phase of my life begin. I had never left England. I set sail on RMS *Strathmore* in January and found myself steaming towards an exotic land, a place of warmth and more importantly offering me a life of freedom and adventure.

It is easy to agree with the notion of shipboard romances as that is what happened to me. I met Alan and the moonlit nights in the Indian ocean, the magical flying fish and sound of the sea led me to agree to marry him at some point in the future. There were many missionaries on-board who thoroughly disapproved of my behaviour. I had a lot to learn and regret a lot of what happened; however, I do recall this as being a rather wonderful time in my life...

I sailed past the Rock of Gibraltar, through the Suez Canal, and in Port Said I went ashore for my first experiences of the East: the

The ship to India

Gibraltar

colours and smells took my breath away. Men and
women in long, flowing colourful robes, palm
trees, monkeys and stalls laden with fruit and
spices, the likes of which I had never seen
before.

Suez Canal

At last four weeks later on 30 January 1948
I saw rising out of the early morning mist the
Gateway to India, built in 1911 for the visit
of King George V and Queen Mary. Behind it like
an extravagant wedding cake was the sumptuous
Taj Mahal Hotel.

Everyone was excited, gangplanks were
lowered, luggage offloaded and coolies swarmed
about to help. We were all dispatched to a

grubby, dark shed which was the Customs House where paperwork was checked and stamped by a great number of officials. I soon realised you needed infinite patience to survive in India.

Surprisingly the streets of Bombay were deserted: I was expecting a mass of humanity. News quickly spread that Mahatma Gandhi had been shot dead in Delhi that day so everyone was huddled around their wireless sets. There was a huge sigh of relief that it was not a Muslim but a right-wing advocate of Hindu nationalism, as that could have doubled the bloodbath. His ashes were later scattered at sea in the Bay of Bombay: little did I realise when writing this that my family returned some of my ashes here... "How extraordinary," she would have said!

Bombay's pavements were covered with sleeping people, men taking baths with their clothes on, beggars maimed, dead cats, rats, and rubbish: it was initially a little alarming for me. However, my most comforting memories are the sounds of dawn – first the pigeons cooing, then the dogs barking, cockerels crowing, and black crows cawing. Later the local Dhobi wallahs slapping their washing on stone slabs, splat, bang, splat as every button was broken in the effort of rendering the clothes spotless, although a little more ragged. The sounds would swell with voices of the vendors selling their wares, the Muslim call to prayer and the continuous honking of horns and tinkling of rickshaw bells. A cacophony of sounds imprinted on my memory for ever.

I had grown up with little sentimentality and quickly realised that here in India life and death is always apparent and acceptable with no embarrassment about either. Suffering, poverty, pain and sickness were part of everyday existence, something to be dealt with, not avoided. You can help where possible, but life must go on: you didn't waste time or emotion on the vastness of suffering that made up a great deal of India and still does today. The political madness and corruption that prevail cannot alter the spirit of the place. On the surface is benign chaos, but the service is gracious, and the smiles genuine. More important are the people: conversations are started at every opportunity, children cuddled, food shared. An acceptance that there is more beyond our need in the West for high achievement. I like to think that I instilled this attitude to life in my children.

My very long train journey three days, from Bombay to Calcutta, made me realise how big the world is. (More about Indian train travel in my Delhi diaries.) I was met in Calcutta by Ted from DGH (Dr Graham's Homes) where I was going to be teaching. Alan, who was still with me, insisted I stay and meet his friends and that he would see me to the train for Siliguri. I regret my ignorance of how a young lady should behave in India, that allowed me to hug and kiss openly, so the first impression I made on other folk was not a good one. Enough said about that romance: I didn't see Alan again for two years.

From Siliguri I changed to the narrow-gauge single-track "toy train" to Darjeeling, taking seven hours to cover 88 km. Built in 1879 by British engineers, the legacy now has UNESCO World Heritage status. The track zigzagged, looped and twisted its way up the hillside parallel to the road frequently (crossing it over 100 times, I was told) and stopping the traffic.

On one side there was a sheer drop to the Teesta River valley, and on the other a hillside covered in the most amazing flowers I had ever seen. Purple, yellow and white orchids, Sikkim lilies and bushes dripping with wild yellow raspberries. Luckily it was the dry season so there were no landslides blocking the track as happened many times in the monsoons. Passengers who couldn't afford the fare clung to the roof, but the train was so slow there was no danger of them falling into the ravine below. At Kurseong, 7,400 ft above sea level, there was a stop for hot, sweet chai and to stretch legs. I now felt truly in the mountains, Tibetan prayer flags fluttering, forests of maple, chestnut, pear and cherry trees and cardamom plants. More layers of clothing and shawls were added before chuntering down to Darjeeling at 6,700 ft. Now rhododendrons and magnolias appeared with a view of Tiger Hill, a unique place to see the sunrise over the Himalayas. No tunnels were built so all could enjoy the scenery. Memories of the views of the majestic snowy peaks of the Himalayas and Kanchenjunga, the smell of pine and eucalyptus trees, stayed with me throughout my life.

I shall never forget my arrival in the foothills of the Himalayas in West Bengal and the incredible drive to Kalimpong and DGH situated on Deolo Hill, twisting and turning on the track, with a driver who seemed to have a death wish, but as always in India we arrived with only minor mishaps along the way. Kalimpong is 4,000 ft above sea level and the climate is like the best English summer, the steep hillsides covered with tea plantations and trees, and football pitches are literally dug out of the hillside. There were no cars in the town, only rickshaws and ponies which cost two rupees for and hour to go wherever one wanted. Mount Everest and Kanchenjunga could be seen on a clear day. Amazing: I cannot believe I am here.

How can there be so much space in the world and such extraordinary beauty? I remember just sitting for days gazing at the views. Everything was new and exciting.

I was taken to my new home in a cottage surrounded by exotic flowers, in the school grounds with another teacher, 40 children and a cook and sweeper, and soon settled in.

I was teaching a class of 11-year-olds in English but I learnt Hindi as well. I felt very fortunate to be in such a lovely place but wanted to teach seniors. Well, the other geography teacher became unwell and had to return to the UK so I was ready to take over her job, so the Lord knew I should be needed and sent me at the right time. Thankfully she recovered from spru (whatever that was I don't remember now). One of my best memories was being able to read by moonlight and walk under the starlit sky. Kite-flying competitions on

Dr Graham's Homes,
the school,
Kalimpoor

View from my
classroom!

the roof were made more exciting by crushing light bulbs and mixing with sugar powder bought from the bazar and sticking this to the kite strings. Kite flights would ensue to cut the opponents' kites down. Rewinding the kite string was a special skill so that you did not cut your hands to pieces.

But I also had to experience the monsoon rains, the continual mists, the mould on leather shoes and the silverfish that consumed my books. Illnesses like tummy bugs, influenza and chickenpox were all caught by most of the staff and pupils. Bugs and insects were part of everyday life, along with snakes in the bathroom and swimming pool, and monkeys stealing through open windows. We eventually persuaded the workshop to fix netting on the windows. At night hundreds of flying foxes (fruit bats) filled the sky: avoiding being bitten was recommended as they can transfer viruses to humans. They roosted in the banyan, tamarind and fig trees in the grounds.

I had a wonderful 3 years teaching there with two hiking expeditions to Sikkim and travelling back to Calcutta for school holidays with other teachers and 80 noisy children to be deposited with their relatives.

TREKKING IN SIKKIM
MAY 1948

Perhaps it would be as well to quote the official handbook:

"Sikkim, or Dejong as it is known to the neighbouring peoples, is a small protected native state lying to the north of the Darjeeling district of Bengal In India. It forms a wedge between its two larger neighbours, Bhutan and Nepal, on the east and west, while to the north lies the Plateau of Tibet. Sikkim measures only 65 miles from north to south, and 45 miles from east to west, but within its confines is to be found some of the finest mountain and ravine scenery in the world."

Lest you wonder what trekking involves, I had better explain that briefly, too.

The hardiest of people take tents and numerous coolies and go to all kinds of out of the way places, but less ambitious ones, like ourselves, make use of the Dak Bungalows for sleeping. These are usually comfortable wooden or stone houses, supplied with furniture, including mattresses on the beds, cutlery and crockery (oddly assorted), where anyone can stay for Rs 3 per night (a rupee is worth about 1s/6d). The bungalows were really built for Sikkim officials inspecting various parts of the country, and each has a chowkidar (caretaker) who looks after the bungalow and lights the fire for cooking.

Tibetan Beggar woman

You take all your own sheets, blankets etc. with you, and all your food. This is all carried on bedding rolls and boxes either by coolies or on the backs of mules.

We had mules because they are very much cheaper. Normally one takes servants, too, but we felt this was an unnecessary expense, so I did the cooking and we shared the sweeping and cleaning between us.

For the first two days we shared two riding horses and then we walked for the rest of the time. Four of us went, Sheila and Ruby, who teach at the Homes with me, and Betty, who teaches in the Scottish mission down the hill.

SATURDAY, MAY 21ST

We had a hectic rush but finally managed to get off in the station wagon at 9 a.m. On arrival at the bazar we transferred into an extremely rickety mail bus. This had been due to leave at 9.30 but owing to a change in the times of the postal services it would not depart until 1 p.m. so we relaxed in an anticlimax. At 1.15 we left the bazar, and at 1.18 we stopped outside the post office for a further three-quarters of an hour while the mail was collected!! At last we really set off and rattled down the hill past the turning to Sikkim and over the Teesta Bridge and wasted a further half an hour shunting backwards and forwards picking up and depositing mail. Finally we recrossed the bridge and set off for Gangtok, the capital of Sikkim.

The Mail Bus

The valley of the river Teesta

Light rain began to fall and the road wound up and down beside the rushing, muddy Teesta River through the forests and looking down on rice fields. Many of the trees were rubber trees and had scarred trunks showing where they had been tapped during the Second World War when the supplies from Malaya had been captured by the Japanese. There were birds and butterflies flitting about and one man was sheltering from the rain under two huge leaves. Five or six landslides were being cleared off the roads and we lurched over these often hovering perilously near a sheer drop to the raging torrents below! Whenever we had to pass bullock carts it was always on the narrowest part of the road and we whizzed round one corner and nearly collided with a red lorry coming equally speedily in the other direction. These buses resemble a box on wheels and if everything had not rattled happily against everything else, the whole machine would have fallen to pieces. Twice we had to stop while the driver got out and disappeared under the bus with a piece of string which he used to tie vital parts of the engine together.

On reaching the frontier we had to show our passes and sign in two books, as no Europeans are allowed to enter Sikkim without passes. We eventually saw the lights of Gangtok (5,800 ft up) at 7 p.m. and were deposited together with four strong, wooden boxes, 2 bedding rolls, and 2 kerosene (paraffin) tins filled with 20 loaves of bread, beside in the road near the track leading to the house of the friend with whom we were to spend the night.

It had taken us 10 hours to cover 50 miles, and our spirits were dampened even further when we were told that the contractor (the man who orders the mules etc.) had forgotten that we were coming and so we should not be able to leave early the following morning as planned. However, one of the main things one has to learn in India is patience, infinite patience, and never to be surprised at anything that happens!!!

SUNDAY, MAY 22ND

The rain tippled down all night but the morning dawn was bright and clear with the deep green of the hills, the fluffy mist in the valleys, and in a gap, the shining whiteness of the Kangchenjunga range made the mountains seem very near. We waited hopefully till 10 a.m. but there was no sign of a contractor, muleteer or mule, so we set off to the bazar. Sunday is market day so the bazar was crowded with people bargaining, bartering, buying and selling: there were Nepalis, Sikkimese, Tibetans, Lepchas, colourful costumes and plenty of

noise and smells, as is common in all Indian bazars. We met plenty of people who had seen the contractor, Rin Sing, for whom we were looking, but he had always just gone somewhere else and in the end we gave up and decided to go to his house after dinner.

So after a sandwich lunch Betty and Ruby went off to a Nepali service and Sheila and I climbed 4 miles uphill – at least we were told it was 4 miles but it seemed more like 2: measurement of distances is a bit haphazard among the locals. Rin Sing of course was out, so we sat on his stone wall surrounded by an assortment of children, cats, dogs, calves, horses, pigs and chickens, and resorted to prayer. After a while it started to rain, and as the only available cover by the woodpile was alive with ants we went up to the first-floor verandah and for $3\frac{1}{2}$ hours we continued to wait reading, writing and trying to get used to the smell, whether due to horses, rabbits or unwashed children we never discovered, but it was pretty overpowering. At last the contractor arrived full of apologies and excuses on account of the political situation etc. He promised us mules for the morrow and almost as he spoke there came a halloo from up the khud (hillside) and down came two Tibetan muleteers. A long discussion on the usual lines followed in Tibetan, arguments as to prices, reluctance, etc. followed by a gradual winning over. This went on with great volubility, if there is such a word, for 30 minutes and then the bargain was made just as everyone had known that it would be from the beginning. Why these folk take such a long time to decide things is quite beyond us, but it is all part of the national make-up and India would not be the same without it. Finally we paid over most of the money we possessed and, through a misunderstanding on our part, sealed the bargain with a drink of murwa which tasted vaguely like cider and is milky in appearance; it is made from millet and is stored in hollow bamboo tubes.

We returned to spread the glad news to the others and retired to bed hoping to see the mules on our doorstep in the morning.

MAY 23RD

At 7.20 a.m. the muleteer arrived together with 2 brown mules, one brown and one grey horse. We were already wide awake, having been serenaded lustily but untunefully by three Tibetans at 6 a.m. The muleteer picked up all our boxes which we were sure were too heavy, loaded them up

The start of the trek

without a word and went off grinning to the tune
of the jingllng mule bells. At 9 a.m. two hefty
riding ponies arrived. The day brightened, the
sun shone, and we jogged along, riding and
walking alternately for three-quarters of an
hour each – no, perhaps 'jogged' is not the
right word, we ambled along, with the horses
determined to walk on every single piece of
grass they saw, even if it meant going twice
as far. One could hardly blame them as the
road was steep and roughly cobbled. We soon
discovered other peculiarities of the horses:
first their determination to follow a zigzag
course; secondly, how they liked to walk on the
very edge of the road particularly when there
was a sheer drop of hundreds of feet below;
thirdly, how they went their own way independent
of which way we pulled the reins, stopped when
they felt like it and walked either head to tail
or head to stirrup, causing the one in front to
wonder when she was going to feel a bite out
of her calf. Considering that none of us had
much experience in riding horses, we managed
very well, for the horses shied at everything,
mules, cows, pigs and the solitary car which we
saw. We had interested stares from, the people
we met (you can stare as much as you like in
India without being thought rude), greetings

of "salaams", and even a tongue poked out which is the Tibetan way of greeting. The Tibetan men that we met had long, matted hair twisted up on their heads, shirts, old trousers, and their thick woollen coats which they need at higher altitudes were tied round their waists. They also wear knee-high leather boots lined with wool. The women's hair was longer and they wore loose ankle-length dresses with long-sleeved blouses and beautiful, multi-coloured, striped aprons. They wear the same type of boots.

The scenery was glorious. The road wound along the hillside through forests which disappeared into a green mist of young bamboos and undergrowth-filled space below and shot up to hidden heights above. Creepers were entwined round all the trees and these were overgrown with moss, making grotesque shapes; the hillsides, rocks, and plants were dripping with moisture and had it not been for the temperature, which was very pleasant, we could easily have imagined that we were in an equatorial forest. Waterfalls cascaded down the hillsides and sometimes the mist swirled up round us.

Gradually the road became steeper and the hillsides rougher and rockier, and among the boulders the yaks were grazing. I was rather disappointed in these animals as I expected them to have longer hair and to look less like cows, but I expect they have thicker coats in Tibet.

The road!

*Buddhist prayer wheels, turned
by the force of water*

We ate our lunch in the middle of the road as the minute we approached the grass leeches started to loop their way towards us. Leeches look something like this and are all sizes from 1/2 inch to 4 inches long. They live on blood and attach themselves to you, suck your blood, and when they are full they drop off. You cannot pull them off, but if you carry a bag of salt with you and touch them with that, they will drop off at once.

By 2.30 p.m. we had reached our first dak bungalow at Karponang, at 9,500 feet up. The bungalow was large and we had a snack of tea, bread, butter, jam, cheese, Marmite, chocolate cake and biscuits when we arrived. Later we had supper – barley soup, sausages, mash, onions, peaches, plums, blancmange, coffee, fudge, sweets, biscuits and lychees (a delicious tropical fruit, tasting like grapes). We went to bed early in readiness for an early start.

MAY 24TH

We left at 7.45 a.m. in pouring rain. However, the mist lifted now and then so we could see the scenery and occasionally the sun broke through. We started out round a horseshoe bend where the road was cut into the mountainside

and supported by stakes. The road rose slowly
and before long, we saw what we had been looking
for: rhododendron trees, scarlet, crimson,
flame, yellow and white, in masses of colour
on the almost vertical hillsides above and
below us.

The road to Carponary

The view at Carponary on May 24th !!

Large, spotted and striped orchids were growing, primulas, star-shaped flowers, and an orange flowering shrub tinted the scene with still more colour. The mist rolled up and away and up again, waterfalls fell into space, scattered their spray on the rocks and flopped into green pools. We met mule trains carrying bales of raw wool and led by the usual cheery Tibetans, saw a few men and women repairing the road, and several children at the scattered settlements, but otherwise we had the world to ourselves. Soon we cut off from the main valley up a smaller one, rising up to 12,500 ft. The sheer beauty of it almost took one's breath away. No longer were there the great heights and depths, but just a pleasant little valley with green grass growing and a river busily singing its way down in the rush of a fall or the swirl of a pool. Great boulders were strewn all over the place and there were craggy, wooded slopes above. There were all the previous colours plus pink, lemon and mauve rhododendrons, too – and we were very thankful that we were now too high for the leeches!!

We saw butterflies and many birds that we did not recognise, including one with a black body, white crown and red fantail that wagged up and down incessantly. We continued to wind upwards. After lunch we saw the waterfall at the head of the valley which showed the start of the Rungpo Chhu (river) which flows from the Tsongo Chho (lake). We almost strained our necks on the last part trying to see round the corner between two high rocks bedecked with prayer flags where the Buddhist travellers and muleteers place a stone in a niche as they pass as an offering to their gods. I forgot to mention that we also saw big prayer wheels in the streams. These are turned by the water so it is a nice, easy way of saying your prayers.

At last we came within sight of the lake, a great, blue lake with the mountains falling into it on one side and a gentler slope where the road wound along beside it: we could see the dak bungalow at the far end and the road winding upwards among the snow. It seems strange that I did not at once realise that this was a cirque (cwm or corrie) but the size of it was so tremendous that I did not recognise it!!! Even now I am not absolutely certain that I am correct, for the far end of the lake which should be the deepest was shallow and had a delta where a stream entered it. The only other explanation is that the mountain at the far end was in fact a terminal moraine and this was merely a type of finger lake – but there is no chance of verifying this now.

Chenpu Lake

The slope behind the bungalow

I went on ahead: the greens and browns of the hills remind one of the Highlands of Scotland for, although you are over 12,000 ft up the lake is completely enclosed by mountains so you are not conscious of the height – apart from headaches which are often experienced here because of the enclosed space and the altitude. The dak bungalow was a lovely, shiny place and there were two roaring fires and a kettle of boiling water awaiting our arrival. After a good supper we retired to bed in down sleeping bags, with blankets and hot-water bottles as it was bitterly cold.

MAY 25TH

We set off at 7.30 with only our own feet to rely on, for the horses had returned the previous day. We intended to do a 14-mile trek including "nipping" up to the Nathu La, a pass 14,150 ft high on one of the most important trade routes into India, and putting our toes into Tibet. It was raining at first but brightened up later on. We were all wearing the maximum amount of clothing, with our pyjamas as an extra layer, and Ruby was wearing a topee with a handkerchief with two holes in it hanging down in front to protect herself from sunburn (she looked like a member of the Ku Klux Klan). The path wound upwards amidst snow and yellow rhododendrons. At the top of the circle of hills surrounding Changu Lake we came into a new valley and through the gap at its southern end we could see range upon range of blue hills interlaced with bands of woolly white clouds and stretching away towards the far distant plains. It was the most incredible view I have ever seen, the sense of space and distance was so great that one felt as if it must be a view from an aeroplane rather than on the ground. The sky was pale blue and nearby to the north rose the slopes of another valley, tree-clad in its lowest parts, then covered with grass and rhododendrons; higher up was juniper scrub and the craggy, snow-covered peaks towered above with baby glaciers running down in crevasses between the trees. All one could hear was the murmur of water far below, the occasional cry of a bird or the tingle of a mule bell – one felt enclosed by silence – in a way I have never felt before or since. The 'road' consisted of rocks just thrown together in a bumpy mass. One mule train of 35 mules passed us, returning to Tibet laden with food, kerosene and other supplies, and another of 70 mules was coming from Tibet bringing bales of wool.

The ever - welcome cup of tea

Ruby's "mask"

In those days everything that went into Tibet had to go by mule and the journey from Gangtok to Lhasa took 18 days. There were six Tibetans with them with their shirts and coats both tied round their waists. The air was very cold but the sun was very hot when it was out but unfortunately the mist kept rolling up and obscuring the view. Before long, we were able to see the Nathu La pass wedged in between the snowy peaks. It seemed a very long way away.

The road rapidly deteriorated. The track descended amidst waterfalls and over a stone bridge near a dark, forbidding and for some reason eerie-looking lake with ice floating on its surface and then wound up again once more amid the melting snow and rocks scattered over a marshy valley above the level of the previous valley upon which the rivers meandered sluggishly.

At last at 11.20 we arrived at the parting of the ways, one road led gently to the Kapup Dak bungalow, and one led very steeply upwards to the pass. We, rather misguided, took the latter and plodded over the loose boulders. The thaw waters from the melting snow which were also running down the road did not make the trudge any more pleasant! Soon we had climbed above rhododendron level and were able to look out east over a valley at the END of which we were — saw the red roof of the bungalow.

on the way up to the Nata la

The cairn of stone

We thought we had nearly reached the pass, but as we turned the corner we saw that the road went on up and so did we, having to stop occasionally and take great, gasping breaths in order to get sufficient oxygen. To the right of us were two frozen lakes covered with snow, and in front of us was a snowy expanse. We kept thinking, 'Surely round the next corner we shall see the pass', but it was a good many corners before we did, and we could see the cairn of stones separating Sikkim and Tibet. We all had headaches from the altitude, our feet felt like lumps of lead, and the sleet was sheeting down on us, but we were not going to be beaten, so we struggled up the last long slope, where the road was just a mass of ice, got to the other side of the cairn, and actually stood in TIBET. It gave one a great sense of achievement to have arrived at last. We sat on the leeward side of the cairn beneath the prayer flags and offerings of wool left by the muleteers, and endeavoured to find a small area of relative warmth. We were doubtless desecrating a Buddhist shrine but as we had the whole world to ourselves, I am afraid we did not worry overmuch.

Snow lay on every side of us and ahead the road went down the side of a steep, brown

valley and on into the misty space – but we
were unable to catch a glimpse of the sacred
mountain of Tibet which one is able to see from
here on a clear day.

Our mule train

We turned back into the icy wind and by the
time we reached the fork in the road the rain
was pouring down. Then followed a trek that
none of us will ever forget. It was supposed to
be a journey of only 4 miles but it must have

been the longest 4 miles ever. The bungalow was visible round every corner, but the more you walked towards it, the further it seemed to go away, rather like an episode from *Alice Through the Looking Glass*. Looking back on it later, one realised what a beautiful walk it had been. Moorland scenery with shrubs and rhododendrons, their leaves a fresh green; boulders and rocks, everything dripping with rain. There were the silent, snowy peaks all around, and the land over which we were walking was a series of ridges and marshy hollows with lakes gradually being infilled by deltas and vegetation. When the mist finally lifted for good, there was the bungalow on the next ridge BUT there was a deep valley in between. Fortunately the path wound around the slope instead of straight up and down, and primulas and yellow starflowers grew in profusion beside the path, while the tall pine trees which were able to grow in the shelter of the valley were festooned with pale green creepers so that it looked as if someone had forgotten to remove the Christmas decorations. The path led to a wooden bridge over a magnificent waterfall which flowed from a hidden lake above. The sun came out and down the valley was a sparkling lake in which were reflected the tall spires of the trees. Waterfalls dropped into space and bounced off the rocks in a film of shining whiteness. The road climbed up again past moss-covered rocks and over babbling burns until at last the bungalow was reached. There were two blazing fires to greet us as our muleteer had arrived many hours before. How grateful we were for them, and after half an hour's complete rest and a few large spoonfuls of Dextrosol (glucose) we were fully revived. There was an interested audience of Tibetans while I cooked the supper, for not only do they rarely see Europeans but only very rarely indeed do they see Europeans who do their own work!! Everything we did amused them for they have a great sense of humour.

We went to bed early with hot-water bottles, a good fire blazing in the hearth with the wood crackling happily, and the firelight flickering on the ceiling.

MAY 26

We awoke at 6.30 to the usual palaver of repacking and getting the mules off. Then after a good breakfast of bacon, fried eggs, fried bread, tomatoes, toast, marmalade, fruit and custard, the others set off for a walk towards the Jelep La (but not over it, we felt we had done enough 'nipping' up for the time) and I wrote up my diary.

At 12 noon we set off to the Natang Dak bungalow, a nice, short stroll after our efforts of the previous day. The rain had cleared and it was only drizzling slightly as we set off up the rough road. I think it is almost impossible for an English person to visualise what the surface of these roads is like. We threw snowballs about and slid down snowdrifts. Thence we looked down into space. What we should have seen and later did see were the Derby Downs, the scene of fighting between the British and the Tibetans. I think it was over a dispute about boundaries when the British were responsible for the safety of Sikkim. There is a war memorial to them in Natang. Many bandits are to be found on this stretch of road and we were rather disappointed not to encounter any of them. We were able to take shortcuts through the juniper scrub, and soon saw the bungalow at the top of a hill (we were beginning to wonder if the roads in Sikkim ever went downhill). As we went lower we were walking on soft, springy grass starred with mauve and white anemones, mauve primulas, and yellow 'dewdrops'.

Towards the Jelep La

*The handsome
"Chowkidar and our
silent mulateer*

The bungalow was very substantial with double windows, a wide verandah, ample space in the rooms and a kitchen connected to the building by a covered way (it is very inconvenient on rainy nights when you have to splosh to the kitchen). The chowkidar was very handsome with twinkling eyes, a lovely smile, and his pigtail wound round his neck. I was quite overwhelmed with offers of help in the kitchen!!! We went out to see the sunset for it was the first time the sky had been clear at this time of the day. We saw the pale orange and pink on the palest of blue skies, the silhouetted mountains with each pine tree clear and black, our brown road stretching back into the darkness and below us a rushing river bounding out of sight into the cotton wool mounds of cumulus clouds also below us. Beyond them were rolls of stratus clouds with the dark blueness of hills between. At our feet the village of Natang huddled together, stone houses with wooden roofs held on with large stones lest the wind should blow them away. The telegraph poles, the only telephone link from India into Tibet (over the Jelep La), stood up like sentinels.

We spent a pleasant evening relaxing round the log fire, talking, writing and reading. Many of the bungalows had a good selection of magazines (in English) with short stories.

MAY 27

The day dawned beautifully but the whole of the rest of it was swathed in thick mist. However, although we could not see into the far distance there was sufficient beauty all around us for us to thoroughly enjoy it all. Our 'guidebook' said 'a steep climb down'. We left at 7.20 and at 9 we were still going up! There were the loveliest rhododendrons and it was a good while before we reached the much-talked-of 'Sikkim/ Cobbles' by which we had to descend 6,000 feet in 6 miles with an average gradient of 1 in 5 but much steeper in parts.

This may not sound particularly difficult, but you try going endlessly down a road made of lumps of stone with spaces between. The shortcuts were either a mass of loose stones or slippery red earth. We had all taken the precaution of putting cotton wool in the toes of our boots for all one could do was gravitate downwards. Incidentally, comfortable footwear is the most essential part of one's equipment: American Army surplus canvas boots with rubber-based soles are ideal. None of us suffered from blisters.

NATANG

The war memorial in the centre distance

The road down

The village with the dark bungalow in the foreground

Rhododendron trees

The vegetation on our descent changed from bleak, barren hills to shrubs and grassland, and then to tropical forest. We met a few ascending mule trains, frequently stopping for a rest and panting frantically. We were very thankful that we were not going their way.

It was rather eerie walking down on the stones with the grotesque shapes of trees and moss-covered rocks looming up out of the whirling whiteness. Sedonchen Bungalow was built on the side of the hill so that the ground floor on one side was the first floor on the other. We had a supper of dhal soup with onions, pulao, curry, beans, prunes and blancmange. In the evening we thought of the 17-mile trek ahead of us tomorrow.

MAY 28

We set off at 7 a.m., walking down the now familiar cobbles. It was still misty and we hurried along quickly for as soon as we stopped the leeches started to loop their way towards us. We crossed raging torrents by bamboo bridges and scrambled up slippery slopes. It felt wonderful to be walking on soft forest paths again. At the village of Lingtan the steep descent ended and the road meandered along beside the river to Rungli where there was a filthy, dirty bazar. It was very hot here as we were only 2,700 ft above sea level. We crossed the river by a long suspension bridge which was being negotiated simultaneously by a train of mules from the other side; the effect

was like that of being on a rough sea. On our
final uphill stretch we were accompanied by the
village schoolmaster who wanted to practise
his English. His pay is Rs 50 per month (£5).

THE ROAD TO ARITA

The suspension bridge

Terraced Slopes from the bungalow

It was an interesting walk for there were many crabs that lolloped and scuttled sideways as we approached, trees with trunks that looked as if they had been daubed with green paint, and people ploughing their fields and planting them. As one mounted the ridge one could see valleys and wooded heights stretching into the distance. At last we reached the top and saw the dak bungalow below us. In the evening we could see the lights of Darjeeling twinkling in the sky and we began to feel that we were nearing home.

This was the only place where we had been bothered by flies but a little D.D.T. soon settled them.

SUNDAY MAY 29

This was our day of rest and we consumed large meals using up some of our hoarded stores. Everything had lasted very well, and it was only the bread which had gone mouldy everywhere except in the middle.

Pedong Bazar

The local tea shop

The hills of "home"

MAY 30

As usual we left early and had a pleasant walk down to Rhenok, the frontier of Sikkim, and then followed a very long climb up to Pedong. The road itself was vastly superior to many of the others but the tremendous heat was most exhausting. Water could not be drunk until it had been sterilised by using special tablets which take 20 minutes to become effective. However, we reached Pedong in the end and consumed quantities of tea in the local tea shop (one has this rather soupy mixture in somewhat dirty glasses but it really tasted good after that climb). The local inhabitants gathered around as usual and the local policeman brought us the book to sign to say we had re-entered India. We visited the homes of some Nepali girls known to Betty. In the first house we were given 2 hard-boiled eggs each, a huge plate of new, white bread and quantities of tea. In the next we had omelettes, French toast and more tea. After we had sung a hymn with the family and had prayer (a custom followed whenever one visits the homes of Christians in this land) we found great difficulty in managing the shortcuts over yet another ridge and we were thankful that the last part of our journey was along a path where many streams ran across the way so we could cool our sweating brows. We went through the cinchona plantations (the bark of this tree is used in the preparation of quinine) and stayed the night in a house belonging to one of the managers. We were certainly back in civilisation, what with proper baths, a set dinner table and beautiful china, as well as clean sheets.

MAY 31

I left the others in bed while I set off at 6.30 a.m. to show the mules the way to the Homes. It was a good road all the way, first through the forest and then along the ridge which was so familiar. It felt good to arrive back leading the mules with their bells jingling away merrily. The muleteer was paid and started on his journey back to Gangtok.

So ended our first Sikkim trek, but we hope to go on another next year.

We only walked 85 miles but we had achieved the aim of getting into Tibet, even if it was only a few yards!!!

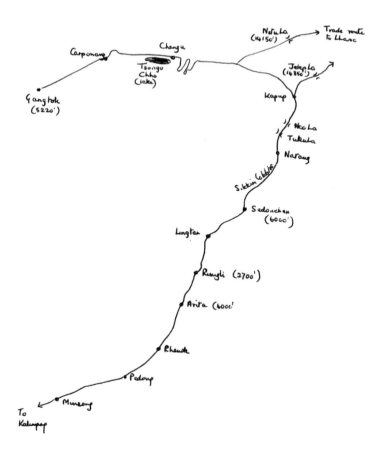

DIARY
1948

AGRA DELHI LUDHIANA
DIARY OF MY HOLIDAY 1948-1949

SATURDAY DECEMBER 11

We, that is four staff and 79 extremely excited
and rowdy boys and girls, left the Homes at 10
a.m. in two buses and one truck – the latter of
so is of course occupied by all the big boys. We
rattled and bumped down to Geillekola, avoiding
the dogs, mules and bullocks. There we stood
for about two hours watching the trains playing
shunting. Eventually the train got all its
various bits attached and then we piled into
the toy train. The method of movement of the
small train is quite unique. It jerks forward
in leaps and bounds and squeaks mournfully
around all the bends, and at Riang, which is

the terminus of the rope railway which brings up most of the stores for Kalimpong, the train created a slight diversion by coming off the rails altogether. This excited a large crowd of Indians but the train was soon levered back onto the rails again and once more we chugged off. There were a few more minor incidents on route – we had frequent stops to give the engine a drink and the engine driver a wash. Then at Sevoke some Tibetan women dumped themselves in the front of our train and firmly refused to budge. In the end the only way to move them was to shove them out amidst screams and yells.

We left Geillekola at 11.30 a.m. and arrived at Siliguri – only 30 miles away – at 5 p.m. It was just getting dark and we had to cope with small children and trying to get them clean, with luggage, and with getting them all fed on a noisy, crowded station. We travelled, 3rd-class in two carriages, and in ours we had 27 of the bigger boys, some sleepy, some complacent, some lively. The train was due to leave at 7.30 but it was 9.30 before it eventually decided to move.

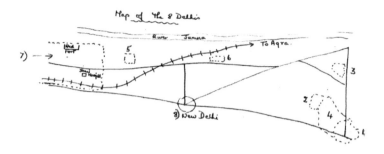

Map of the 8 Delhis

SUNDAY

Midnight on Saturday saw us speeding over the
moonlit plains trying to make up for lost time.
The driver no doubt had the best of intentions,
but he was thwarted by the Customs and by the
signalmen for there were frequent stops. Some
of the boys slept, others, and I, too, were
too uncomfortable and we spent most of the time
gazing out of the window at the moon dancing along
beside us in the flooded rice fields. As the moon
set in sullen orange and the first colours of the
dawn streaked the sky, we passed clankingly over
the mile-long Hardinge Bridge, which spans the
broad Brahmaputra. Soon the teak trees, bamboos
and coconut palms were silhouetted against
the lightening sky, and village huts could be
discerned through the cotton wool blanket of
mist which swathed the ground.

We arrived in Calcutta 5 hours late and got the children sorted out and delivered to their relations. I and another girl who was bound for the North-West Frontier to do missionary work in Pakistan, spent the day with friends, but despite the thrill of seeing traffic and lights and houses, hearing town noises, and smelling Indian smells (which one gets used to remarkably quickly) I had an attack of 'homesickness' for Kalimpong.

We managed to get into an Inter Zenana (ladies) compartment on the Delhi Express without much trouble, along with 2 Anglo-Indians and their 5 children and an Indian lady and her 2, so it is relatively comfortable. The train actually started on time and now we are rocking off through the night towards Agra and Delhi.

Incidentally for those who don't know, I'd better explain a bit about travel in India. Now there are only 3 classes as in England, but Indian 2nd-class is equivalent to English 3rd, and the 3rd has wooden seats and often is not at all clean. But up to this year and still in Pakistan, there were (and are) 4 classes — 1st, 2nd, Inter and 3rd. Inter is less than 1/2 of the 2nd-class fare, and not too bad, so normally we travel Inter. For instance, the fare from here to Calcutta 2nd-class is

33 rupees (£2 10s) and Inter it is 13 rupees (£1). The new Indian 2nd-class is at Inter Class fare, so it is quite reasonable and often more comfortable than it used to be.

MONDAY

Thank goodness for a good night's sleep, as sleep goes when you have to people bashing on the doors at every station, either to see tickets or to try and get into a carriage which is already comfortably full. I slept on a pile of trunks and apart from a very sore behind felt little other stiffness. At 7 a.m. we reached Patna where there was the usual noise and bustle. It had been a freezing cold night and it didn't really warm up all day, as we were sitting on the shady side of the train.

We swept over the open plains, past rice fields, sugar cane, dhal and grass growing in square patches in the fields. The countryside was dotted with trees and birds flew about – parrots, blue jays, kingfishers, woodpeckers, bulbuls, drongos, egrets, mynas, crows, vultures, and many others that I did not know. On we went by the mud huts of the villages past the goats, bullocks, oxen, cows, buffaloes and camels, the latter heaving themselves

superciliously along in their usual manner.
I had not expected to see any hills at all,
but soon the country became dry and sandy,
and without any cultivation. There were deep
gulleys and the low hills were covered with
bushes. Only cattle and horses grazed here.
Then back into the fertile Ganges valley which
winds broadly through a wide, sandy bed. We went
through Allahabad, a rather pleasant-looking
town, though in the poorer quarters the houses
are all on top of each other as if huddling
together for warmth. You pass women out with
the cattle, weeding in the fields or washing
in the ponds, men talking, driving the buffalo
carts, guiding the ploughs or lying outside
asleep on low bamboo and matting beds – for in
India, as in most other parts of the world, it
is the women who do the most work. Everywhere
you see life, some of it pretty miserable
admittedly, but life nevertheless such as you
never, or rarely, see in England. Even the
sameness of the countryside does not bore you,
for there is always something happening. When
one tries to think of some part of England
that is compatible in any way to the plains of
India, there is only one part that comes to
mind – the real Fenlands of East Anglia. There
you have the same flatness, clumps of trees and

square fields (although these are larger than in India); the difference lies in the air of desolation which is totally absent in India.

7.30 p.m. and we have just arrived at Cawnpore, and undergone an invasion of Punjabi women. We are packed very tightly together and more or less sleeping on each other's laps.

TUESDAY DECEMBER 14

One a.m. saw me alighting at Tundla Junction, looking, I imagine, like some new type of teddy bear, wearing a zipper jacket, top coat, woolly coat on my head, and a large blanket on top of all that. The train to Agra was waiting and I discovered that it was only one hour's journey, although by the time we had finished shunting out of the station and back in again it was 1.45 before we left. I fell asleep on the way. (It is amazing how after a time one can sleep on anything, bare boards, cross-legged on a seat, curled up like a hedgehog: it makes no difference.) I discovered that Agra had three different stations, which wasn't much help as no instructions from Maggie (my school friend married to a Bengali, whom I was going to see) had arrived. I alighted at the third one because I had discovered that there was a waiting room there. Imagine arriving at a freezing cold station at 3 a.m. and having the prospect of staying in an equally cold waiting room for the next few hours. However, I settled down and slept on a wooden bench till 6.30. I left on a tonga (a two-wheeled horse carriage) driven by a very voluble Hindu who spoke a bit of English and was obviously charging me an exorbitant fare, but I was too tired to argue. I arrived just in time for breakfast and found Maggie, her husband, Nipu, with Tupu, their 2-year-old son, and Guria, the 5-month-old baby, all there. Tupu was most intrigued with my European clothes.

I had the pleasure of a most necessary bath, Indian fashion, i. e. you have a bucket of water, pour half of it over yourself, then soap all over, and then empty the rest of the water over yourself. Then I washed my hair and my clothes, which dried very quickly in the hot, dry atmosphere.

The rest of the morning I lazed about, watching the birds, dog, cats, buffaloes, pigs, little, grey striped squirrels, servants and children who all occupied the garden.

We had a very tasty and substantial tiffin of rice, dhal and fish curry followed by kayla (bananas), with haloowa (made of fried

semolina and sultanas) for tea. I was quite
ready to go to bed but we decided to go for a
walk before supper. Having visited the college
principal's wife next door, we wended our way
to the bazar. Our way led through the Hospital
Garden and at first it is rather surprising
to glance up and see four monkeys sitting
on a wall and regarding you with a somewhat
superior expression. But even monkeys become
a natural part of one's environment before
long. It was strange to be back in the midst of
noise again after the quiet (comparative) of
Kalimpong. The jostling crowds, the bicycles
winding precariously along between the tongas
with their shouting drivers and the eckhars
led by gaily decorated horses, all added to
the confusion. The usual little shops lined
the roadsides and the usual smells filled the
air – this was India all right. We went past
bookshops, subjee (fruit and veg) shops, piled
high with all kinds of oranges, pomegranates,
bananas, guavas, cheams (beams), radishes the
size of turnips, past cloth shops, and deeper
and deeper and further and further into the
bazar, full of people and goods – if only one
had a lot of money. We returned in a tonga and
had a large supper – meat curry, vegetables,
chupatis (or 'pulkas' as they are called here):

these are made by mixing atta, which is ground
wheat, into a paste, kneading it for a long
time, cooking in the shape of a small, thin
flat pancake on an ungreased griddle over the
fire, and then holding it in tongs over the
flames themselves so that the hot air gets
in and it inflates. This was followed by a
nightcap of hot milk with sugar, a banana and
a chupati in it, rounded off with some (chilgoo
ja) nuts, which resemble miniature torpedoes,
taste of cinnamon and smell of pine trees.

WEDNESDAY

Nipu and I had been fortified by a tea of
pukkoeas (powdered dhal, known as besum, is
mixed into a paste and into it are dipped
slices of raw potato, spinach, pumpkin, onion,
etc.; these are fried until crisp in deep fat,
ghee, or mustard oil). Lovely. We set off to
see the Taj Mahal by moonlight. We decided to
walk there as it was very cold. First we went
through the streets of a bazar, crowded and
noisy, with shuttered buildings, carved stone
balconies, a family squatting round a fire made
with dried cow's dung, their faces glowing red
as they glanced towards us, along a street of
shoe shops, where leather was hanging in weird

stiff sheets and men were machining or nailing on soles. Bicycles, tongas and eckhars rattled along the streets and the air was filled with noise and smoke and dust. Soon we came to Agra Fort, a grim, forbidding mass on our left, while opposite were the lights of and chimneys of the big power station, and in the centre the outlines of a refugee camp. The fort was built in the time of the Moghuls, and here Akbar spent some of his life in the domed palace within. Even in the moonlight the strength of those walls was apparent. First there is a moat on three sides, while the Jumna flows on the other, then a low, red sandstone wall, proceeded by a higher one of great thickness, with arrowslits and a rounded top instead of the usual castellated effect. It is so huge that one feels completely dwarfed beside it, for it must be about a square mile in area. Within is the Palace and here Shah Jahan lay when he ended his days imprisoned by his son Aurangzeb, and gazed towards the Taj where his wife lay buried. Some of the stone for these edifices was transported by elephant, but much of it came by the rivers, which were India's chief means of transport before the railways were built. The moat is now part of the open sewer system of Agra, so the smell can be imagined.

Entrance Gate to Taj Mahal

Our Christmas Tree at Agra

Taj Mahal

Pearl Mosque - Agra Foot

*Entrance Gate to Akbar's
tomb Secundra*

Akbar's Tomb

We walked on through the Government Park towards the Taj which I saw once or twice in the distance, looking like a ghost in the moonlight. At last we reached the outskirts – first you have the outer court where there are the tombs, each a miniature Taj in itself, of various relatives; and the long arcades in Hindi architecture where visitors used to stay in those days. You pass through the great archways and then come to the outer wall of the inner court. Here there is a most magnificent gateway with minarets and small domes on top, and the path leads through a domed hall and up to steps looking out on what must surely be one of the most wonderful sights in the world. The moon gleamed on the still waters of the long canals with fountains in the centre, the small, straight cypress trees stood like dark sentinels on either side, while in front was the white and silent Taj, huge and magnificent, seeming but a few feet away. We walked towards it, me almost falling in the water because I could not take my eyes off it, and as we walked it seemed almost to recede instead of getting nearer. Then we stood beneath the first of the marble walls above which the Taj is built; up some steps and onto the next terrace of sandstone and marble where we had to put on overshoes because this place is holy to the Muslims. Then up more marble steps and onto the wide terrace with a high circular minaret at each corner. You stand there and the height of the building almost takes your breath away. You stand there and gaze up at the Persian writing of the Koran inlaid into the marble in touchstone and the wonderful flower designs in semi-precious stones such as jade, lapis lazuli, goldstone, coral, onyx etc. and the carving in the pure marble of which the whole building is made. It is not difficult to understand why it took 22 years to build and cost, even in those days, rupees 60,000,000 (it would be six times as much today). In the light of the moon the stones shone and glistened and gave an unearthly beauty to the scene. We went inside through the entrance hall floored with black designs done by Chinese craftsmen, walls with carved marble slabs decorated with inlaid stones, to the central part of the great 80-foot-high, central dome where the echo of your voice lasts for 15 seconds, and saw the tomb of Mumtaz Mahal with Shah Jahan's beside her. He intended to build himself a similar tomb of black marble on the other side of the Jumna, but since he was imprisoned he was not able to. Then down a marble corridor into the vaults where the actual bones are supposed to be in tombs similar to the ones above. We walked round the outside and every view of the Taj brought fresh beauty, particularly in symmetry of design. The wide, white waters of the Jumna flowed peacefully along behind.

Coming away, we walked through Taj Ganj, a suburb of Agra renowned for its gazak. The scene was typically Eastern, and with the small, shuttered shops, the tiny windows, the cry of a carpet seller, the mutter of men around a small fire and the white moonlight shining on the white and red stone buildings, the scene was perfectly set for an adventure story - a sinister cry, a flurrying footstep, a shadow in a doorway - anything might happen. That by the way, is one of the unique things about India, unique in my limited experience: anyway, you never know what is going to happen next. That and the bazars are two of the reasons why it would be difficult to settle down in England again after being out here. We bought the gazak, lovely stuff, long, hard, sweet, nutty and with an indescribable lingering flavour of camphor.

We came back in a tonga to a supper which included jimicand (a brown vegetable resembling a potato in taste, but as big as a football in

original size), cheam (like flat runner beans)
and part of an anah (like a pomegranate, red in
colour and with seeds inside covered in a pulp
which you suck off. The flavour is of grapes,
port wine, and syrup mixed together).

You may be interested in the legend about
the building of the Taj. Mumtaz was in love
with a Persian lad and when she was carried off
to Shah Jahan's harem, he followed her. When
she died, Shah Jahan asked anyone who wanted
to submit designs for a tomb for her. The
Persian lad's design was naturally the best,
but somehow Shah Jahan discovered that he was
her lover, and ordered him to be killed by
being trampled on by wild elephants, His life
was spared, however, but his eyes were put out
so that he would never be able to see the tomb
that he had designed.

THURSDAY

A day eventful only for its food; lunch
included partridge (they only cost about 8d)
and tikkis (rissoles). For tea, we had samosa
(curry patties) and mithai (Indian sweetmeats),
jellabies, and something like trifle and round,
white balls made of milk in a special form, but
tasting like breadcrumbs soaked in honey. Also

there was gaja ka haloowa – a wonderful dish, which you ought to be able to make in England. Carrots are grated and boiled until soft. Then they fried and sugar, milk, nuts are added. For supper there was (kijeree) rice and dhal mixed. Most of the day we lay out and rested under the neem tree in the garden. This is a very useful tree in the plains, for not only do its leaves provide thick shade, but its twigs are also used as toothbrushes and toothpaste combined by the Indians. Animals feed on its leaves and for skin diseases you can either fry the leaves and eat them, or cook them and bathe in the juice.

In the evening we went to a college concert. I imagine it was rather typical of India in that it started an hour late and there were very long intervals in between each item. There were rhythmical Indian dances, by men with rows of bells round their ankles which clanged in time to the music, and musical items on harmonium, violin and tubla (drums like tom-toms which are played dexterously with the fingers).

SUNDAY DECEMBER 19

In the evening we went to a carol service at one of the big churches in Agra. The place was crowded with Indians young and old, and I only saw half a dozen other Europeans. It was a big church, painted cream, and behind the altar was an orange-gold wall hanging. On high ledges on either side of the altar along the front of the church, small, white candles were burning and then filled the chancel with light. Carols were sung in Urdu and English. To hear 'O, come all ye faithful' sung in Urdu was a wonderful experience: the rafters absolutely rang with the sound. In a town which is a centre of Hinduism, this evidence of the following that Christ had was very encouraging.

We had a pigeon each for supper, costing 5d!

THURSDAY DECEMBER 23

Not much has happened during the week, for Maggie has been ill all the time, although we paid some very interesting visits to various Indian friends of hers. I'd been wanting to meet Indians and get into a real Indian atmosphere for a long time, and now I have my wish.

We went to the Women's Association of Agra College Annual Day. There are only 40 women to 1,600 men – reminiscent of Cambridge. It was a good entertainment and vastly superior to that of the men previously. For one thing it started only $\frac{1}{2}$ an hour late. No boys were present because they have not yet got used to this emancipation of the women of India which is now in progress and consequently don't know how to behave. There were songs, instrumental items, tableaux from the stories of Rama and Sita, a one-act play in English, which was amusing and well-acted, even though they could not manage the Cockney accent. The item I liked best was a Gujarati dance which about 10 of them did together. The dance was good but it was the marvellous saris which attracted my attention. There was a grass green sari with a wavy gold edge, a pale blue with a broad silver border, two transparent ones with deep wine-coloured underskirts, a creamy, filmy one with gold embroidery, a scarlet silk and many others – costing over rupees 150 each, unfortunately.

CHRISTMAS EVE 1948

No word from Alan, but I expect he will turn up sometime. We've made the drawing room look very Christmassy with decorations, greenery and a Christmas tree.

CHRISTMAS DAY

My first Christmas Day in India! In the morning I went to a C of E service attended by about 18 people and conducted by a man with a most mournful voice who said, 'Behold I bring you glad tidings of great joy,' as if he had a number of very severe internal pains.

However, we had a proper Christmas dinner of chicken and Christmas pudding.

In the evening some of the neighbours came in and Maggie and I dressed up as a pantomime horse and then I transformed myself into an Irish-voiced replica of Father Christmas. You should have seen the look of complete mystification on Tupu's face.

Supper was partly supplied by the neighbours next door, so it was a massive repast.

MONDAY DECEMBER 27

I decided it was time I saw something of Agra, and since Maggie was still ill, I went alone.

The road to the Taj through the park was glorious. Water was streaming down the hillocks and running over the grass, glinting so brightly in the sunlight that it dazzled you. The details of the Taj could be seen better in daylight, but I preferred it by moonlight.

I took a tonga back to the fort and procured someone who was labelled 'First-Class Guide' (because he could speak English).

We went first into the Diwan-i-Aam (Court of Public Audience), walking along by the red sandstone walls 4½ feet thick and 75 feet high. Below this is a lower wall 45 feet high. To get to the court you go through the Akbari Gate (the fort was built by Akbar, Jahangir, Shah Jahan and Aurangzeb, all of the last three added bits) and into a large courtyard surrounded by arcades on three sides. In the centre is a very deep well, tapping the Jumna and thus assuring the fort of a water supply in times of siege. On the fourth side is a marble-pillared and roofed open hall where the King used to sit and make laws and decrees. On either side of the dais are rooms where the Queen and her ladies could sit, hear what was going on and give advice if they wanted to. Next we went to the Pearl Mosque which was built by Shah Jahan. It has three domes and is made of white marble with beautifully carved arches. Apart from the flower and leaf carving in individual blocks and the Persian writing, Moghul architecture is remarkably simple when compared with the Hindu. From the mosque we went into the courtyard behind the Diwan-i-Aam which was formerly a very deep fish pond, and looked over the far side to a grassy space between the walls which was used for elephant and tiger fights. Through to the Diwan-i-Khas (the Hall of Private Audience) and onto the verandah of the Jessamine Tower where Shah Jahan was kept a prisoner. Most of the rest of the fort is devoted to rooms for women-very many in those days of harems. There are rooms for the princesses, walled-in courtyards and places where they used to play a kind of Ludo, using live slave boys and girls for counters. The next big courtyard is known as the Vinegarden, and is one of predominantly Hindu architecture. Some of the old paintings and decorations have been renovated or copied and they are very beautiful. The pillars and walls here were much more ornate. The building where the Queen used to bathe is domed and arched and all the walls and roofs are covered with small squares of glass which reflect colour and light. It took me a whole hour to walk round – actually it is $\frac{1}{2}$ mile all around the walls but it is not possible to see them all because the Army are in part-occupation.

TUESDAY DECEMBER 28

Today I started off at 9 a.m. to walk to Dayalbagh. It was a lovely day and the road lay out past the jail into the open sandy country with cultivation only along the irrigation canals. The road was hot and dusty but it made the tree-shaded main street of Dayalbagh itself seem even more pleasant. Dayalbagh seems to belong more to a development scheme in England than in India. For here is this community of 5,000 people, living in an area of $5\frac{1}{2}$ square miles of land (including large tracts which are irrigated for agriculture) in good, clean houses surrounded by open greens, with Nursery, Primary and Secondary Education, University, Technical College, Teachers' Training Centre, Hostels, Hospital, Cemetery, Model Dairy Farm, Post Office, Bank, Shops, and their own Industries producing various goods and employing up-to-date methods of workmanship. Dayalbagh is also a religious community, a sect from Hinduism, so there is an additional co-ordinating factor.

It took me $2\frac{1}{2}$ hours to see round it and then we went over the road to the grounds of a similar sect of monastical bent, where they are building a temple to Raja Swami, as they call the founder of their sect, which will rival the Taj when it is completed. However, owing to a lack of funds, they have taken over 40 years to build less than a quarter of it. There is a grand view from the roof to the Taj one way and to Akbar's tomb at Secundra the other, and everywhere the bumpy, brown desert is interspersed with trees and patches of green near the canals. We went to one of their houses for refreshment and talked, mostly about their religion and mine, till it was 3 o'clock and much too late for me to get home for dinner.

I walked back, purchasing a long stick of sugar cane en route; it was longer than I was, and to eat it you cut it into foot lengths, wash it, take off the outer skin, and then with your teeth tear off bits of the fibre, suck out the sugar, and spit out the woody part.

WEDNESDAY

I set out early to St. John's College to meet Miss Gibbs with whom I was going to walk the $3^1/_2$miles to Secundra. She was large and pleasant and talked practically incessantly the whole way. The road is known as Akbar's Royal Road and leads along through an avenue of trees with the ruins of houses and tombs of the Moghul period on either side. The country is so flat that you can see the gate of the tomb a very long way off. As usual there were all sorts of interesting things to look at on the way: a local brickworks, buffalo carts with their huge wheels characteristic of this part of India, ponds and wells, green crops of dhal and yellow crops of mustard, the seeds of which are used for making mustard oil, extensively used for cooking, lighting and keeping the skin and hair healthy in this extremely dry climate. Before long, we were facing the gateway of Akbar's tomb, in predominantly Hindu architecture since he was the first of the Moghuls and much influenced by the people he had conquered.

It is interesting to note that the design of crosses comes into the carving along some of the walls and in the marble screens. One of Akbar's wives is reputed to have been a Christian. I climbed to the top and looked out through windows in the trellis-like marble screens, down over the wooded 'bagh' (park) where the straight-horned deer were feeding, over the high red wall and onto the wide expanse of semi-desert stretching away into the heat haze.

Tank & well nr Secundra

The Plains - from Akbar's Tomb

Bullock carts - nr Secundra

Kanch Mahal - nr Secundra

Me in my sari

I had lunch at the lovely octagonal, verandahed and whitewashed bungalow in the grounds with the St. John's folks who were staying there for a few days. Afterwards, I went to see the Kanch Mahal, a very small building which many people do not know exists. There are the most exquisite carvings on the walls, including one of elephants fighting. Home in a tonga, first of all passing a crowd of langurs, grey black-faced monkeys with long, loopy tails.

SUNDAY JANUARY 2ND

I started the day off by going to a service in Hindustani, following the hymns chiefly because I knew the tunes.

At about 11 o'clock we set off for Fatehpur Sikri, 'we' consisting of Mr. and Mrs. Rae next door, with their 4-yr- and 7-yr-old children, and 2 nephews, aged 19, Mr. and Mrs. Metha, the principal and his wife, their 2 grown-up daughters, and a young doctor, Nipu, Maggie and myself. The road to Fatehpur Sikri is another of the royal roads lined with trees, and our bumpy bus went along, hooting everyone and everything else out of the way, including the red-faced monkeys, who heaved themselves up into the trees and looked down on us as we passed, doubtless making some rude comments. The crops of dhal, sugar cane and mustard we were growing and the winter wheat showed green above the ground. There were various types of wells - some where you heave up a bucket, others where there was a slope up to the well, down which harnessed buffaloes walked, thus pulling up great water containers made of hide. The villages here looked rather as if some giant hand had just thrown them together.

All the houses were made of mud with thatched roofs and, usually, wide verandahs supported by posts or mud pillars. Some of the houses are surrounded by high-walled yards, others have fallen down: the two impressions that one gets are of continual decay and huddled-togetherness. It is a 22-mile journey out there and soon we were able to see the outlines of some of the buildings standing on the crest of the sandstone ridge. We went first to the Dak Bungalow and ate an extremely satisfying Indian dinner sitting cross-legged on durries (mats) and they thought we had better start exploring before we all fell asleep. Fatehpur Sikri is a town which was built by Akbar in the 16th century and then abandoned presumably because the water supply was inadequate. It was fortified and contained houses, mosque,

courts, stables, quarters for his harem etc.
All along the foot of the hill at one side was
a lake which dried up, but you can see its
bounds because the whole area is more fertile
than the surrounding land and at this time of
the year is a bright green with the growing
crops. We walked up past the Treasury and
the Mint and the old stables (Akbar was very
fond of horses) and into the Diwan-i-Aam with
its square Hindu arches and carved pillars.
Nearby is the Diwan-i-Khas where the king held
his Privy Councils, and here the centre of
attraction is a huge, carved pillar supporting
a circular platform where the king's throne
was, so that he felt he was the centre of his
kingdom with all his nobles sitting around him.
We saw some of the draughty-looking double-
decker houses belonging to some of his wives,
although in those days there were curtains of
thick material over the doors. Most of the
carvings on these buildings were done first
on the separate blocks and then they were put
into place with a special sort of mortar that
they don't know how to make nowadays. Anyway,
it has all stood up to the heat and changes of
temperature. Akbar made sure that no one would
go peeping into Jodha Bai's Palace by making
its second entrance, not in line with, but

slightly to the right of, the first. Further on
is the high Elephant Gate, where the elephants
and horses used to make their way into the
town up a steep slope. On the gate are the
remains of huge carvings of elephants, and at
the bottom of the slope is a building which
looks like a lighthouse with guns sticking out
all the way round. Purpose unknown. Before
entering the Jami' Masjid (mosque) we had to
take off our shoes, and we went first to the
small marble tomb of Salim Chishti, one of the
Muslim saints. As one enters the Jami Masjid
there is a tremendous sense of space: all around
is the wide, marble-floored courtyard (it's
lovely walking on marble in bare feet), high
sandstone walls, gates of sandstone and marble
in the centre of each side, with the Buland
Darwaza (Gate of Victory) on the left, and the
entrance to the sanctuary ahead. This small
tomb is on the right and surrounded by carved
marble screens. But inside the actual tomb is
a rectangular platform three feet above the
ground with a flat canopy on top and the whole
thing is covered with hexagons of mother-of-
pearl, kept in place with brass nails. You
imagine something covered with mother-of-pearl
and reflecting all the delicate colours you ever
dreamed of and more beside and you have some

idea of how lovely it is. The Buland Darwaza is a wonderful sight, too, just one single arch towering up 145 feet with a very steep flight of steps up from the bottom making the full height 176 feet. Nearby a man was jumping 80 feet from the wall of the mosque into a well – all for 8 Rs. The mosque itself is the only part which is really Moghul architecture.

After that we walked round the outside of the walls, or rather those of us who still had any energy left did. To go along the road where the elephants, slaves and others wended their way in olden days beside the still waters of the lake and to gaze up on the now partly ruined walls and wonder what it must have been like then, is a thrilling experience, for whether you are young or old the words 'deserted city' conjure up all sorts of pictures in your imagination. We climbed up the 'lighthouse' and decided that the 'guns' were probably the remains of elephants' trunks and this may have been some kind of memorial to them. Who knows? The only unpleasant part of the walk was the passing and the smelling of several skeletons of cattle.

We honked our way home in the gathering darkness, through a bazar, alive as only an Indian bazar can be (doubtless with some small species of animal, too).

Buland Darwaza -
Fathepur Sikri

Jodh Bai's Palace -
Fathepur Sikri

Dewan-i-Am. Red Fort, Delhi

Thro The Rang Mahal - to Dewan-i-
Khas - to the Hammer

Jami 'Masjid - Delhi - Refugees
washing in Foreground

WEDNESDAY

Today once more I set off early to the Itmud-Ud-Daula, a tomb of a nobleman, erected by Jahangir's wife, Nur Jahan (meaning the Light of the World). She was much more businesslike than her husband and he let her run the kingdom for him. I went first towards the fort and then along a road beside the Jumna. There was a cold breeze blowing and it would have been very pleasant walking if there had not been a miniature dust storm as well. Eventually I reached the Jumna Bridge, a very ugly affair and seemingly much too large for the small amount of water that was running underneath. But in the rains all these sandbanks are a swirling mass of muddy water. In the pools left in the riverbed there were turtles swimming about, basking in the sunshine on the side or heaving themselves along on flipper-like feet. Their backs are flattish and I was too far away to see whether they are hard or not. They looked rather like the backs of soles. Near the other side where the river is flowing at present, the dhobis were at work – no wonder clothes washed by them don't last long, when you see the way they slosh them down on the stones as if they were beating a carpet. The bridge itself was crowded with every conceivable type of traffic, from bicycles to buses and including camels. The tomb was easily visible from the road but of course I did not see it and went on cheerfully walking through the dust. Some people told me it was 'ahgay' (in front), others that it was 'peechay' (behind), and finally I walked back to it. Each of the four gateways was in delicately carved and chiselled sandstone and the tomb itself showed the 'feminine touch' very clearly. Its style is Hindu but it is all done in white marble. There is a marble-screened rectangular pavilion on the roof and a little Moghul minaret at each corner. The whole thing is covered in flower designs inlaid with semi-precious stones. The tops of the arches leading into the tomb itself are all carved with various sprays of flowers and the walls are covered with paintings of flowers and other designs. The floors are in marble mosaic. Going home I decided to have some variety and went back a different way. I had a marvellous time wandering around all sorts of bazars and having only a very slight idea of where I was going. The streets were crowded with people and animals and there were so many roads all looking exactly the same that it was like being in a maze. There was a whole row of silversmith shops where they were beating out the bangles and brooches, another of sweetshops where they were making the gazak – there is a long nail outside the shop where they sling the sugary stuff which at this point looks for all the world like a skein of rubber knitting wool: they pull it round, slap it about, twist it up, until it is ready for the next process – I don't know what that is, but finally they flatten it out with wooden mallets used as hammers.

FRIDAY JANUARY 7TH

Here beginneth the story of another priceless day. We discovered that the Grand Trunk Express to Delhi which I was going to catch went at 4.12 a.m. and the next was at 4 p.m. So I decided to go from Agra Fort to Tundla and get the connection. Thus I should arrive at Delhi by 6 p.m. Alas for my hopes I had reckoned without the Indian railways! I got to Tundla Junction all right about 12.30 to discover that the Express from Calcutta had gone but I could catch the Parcel Express at 2.30. So I retired to the waiting room and talked Hindi to a very nice old lady.

2.30 When is the train coming (in Hindi)? Right away

3.00 When is the train coming (in Hindi)? Right away

3.30 When is the train coming (in Hindi)? Right away

4.00 When is the train coming (in Hindi)? Right away

And it actually did. There was only 3rd-class on the train, so I got into a ladies' compartment occupied by 4 soldier's wives and their husbands in the Indian Army. The officials removed the soldiers but one of them came back later on and at subsequent stations more and more females got in so were packed together. I was fed by the soldier's family. Several heated arguments in very rapid Hindi ensued from time to time among the females and at one station a man got in and refused to move, until the soldier unrolled himself and booted the man out without waiting to ask questions. We arrived at Delhi at 11.45 p.m. so I spent the night in the 1st-class waiting room.

SATURDAY.

I started the day with a cold ride in a tonga and an English breakfast. The morning was spent arranging to get some money and visiting the Secretariat in New Delhi to try and get some news of Alan. All I discovered after the obliging little receptionist had phoned up at least six different departments was that Alan had not yet been called for duty.

After dinner I went to the Red Fort in Old Delhi, built by Shah Jahan. Much of it is occupied by refugees and the Army, but the archaeological section is reserved. This fort, being all built by one person and not four, is more beautiful in design and more coherent in arrangement than the one at Agra, but it does not give the same impression of vastness. Originally most of the ceilings were inlaid with gold and silver and the floors were of marble, but the former was looted and the floors had to be replaced by sandstone. The garden was beautifully kept, and the water supply seemed to the be Shah Jahan's chief concern. You go through the Gate and face the Diwan-i-Aam. Inside is the raised platform where the Emperor addressed the people and all round it are the loveliest decorations. The most beautiful are inlaid stones in the shape of birds and with a picture of Orpheus with his lute showing the Italian influence, but the whole place is a mass of inlaid work of intricate design. Across the next wide, grassy stretch you come upon the Rang Mahal, in the centre of which is a fountain in whose bed is a huge, carved lotus. Four streams called the Streams of Paradise ran into this fountain and the water so moved that it appeared as if the petals of the lotus were moving. At either end of the building were two domed rooms with roofs entirely made of glass (most of which has been removed) but even now if you strike a match you can see the reflection in a convex piece of glass at least fifty times. In line with this is the Khas Mahal, a high marble hall with rooms at one end and reconstructed to look as they did in Moghul times. I saw the rich carpets and hangings, walls covered in designs, cushions against which they reclined, and a hookah beside the King's place. The other room was simpler and was used for prayer. You can look through a marble screen and a square opening which used to be decorated in gold and silver, with the painting of the scales of Justice above, to the Diwan-i-Khas, the home of the fabulous Peacock Throne which was six feet long and made of all the precious jewels imaginable, put in the form of a peacock. Here once more is all the simplicity of form and intricacy of design within this form. On to the Hammam (Baths) - talk about a bathroom, you could have a hot hath, a cold bath, a rose water bath, a tepid bath or an oil bath! All in separate places decorated like a palace.

The Moti Masjid (Pearl Mosque) is smaller than the one at Agra but the harmony of the simple arches is lovely. Most of the rest of the Palace is taken up with summer houses and gardens where the water flowed in marble canals beside flower beds and cypress trees. From the surrounding parapet you look out over the grass and trees to the Jumna, here presently just a narrow stream river, and spanned by a magnificent bridge with two storeys, one for cars etc. and one for trains.

Coming back I took a wrong turning and wandered about a mile out of my way around some of the filthiest bazars I have ever seen, though probably they are no worse than some of the slums of London. Actually it is much quicker to walk than to go any other way in bazars because tongas, cars, trams, cycles and bullock carts get themselves into the most wonderful traffic jams in the narrow streets from which they only extricate themselves after a number of people have given a great deal of useless advice and a greater number of people have been quite content to sit back and let the hours go by. Eventually I got to somewhere I knew and I arrived home at 5.30 – very dirty.

Humayun's Tomb

From the Library, Purana Qila
looking to New Delhi

Jantar Mantar, New Delhi The
Sundial

Government House, New Delhi

Secretariat, New Delhi

Memorial Arch & George V
Statue - New Delhi

MONDAY

In the afternoon I went to New Delhi to see an exhibition of Indian art and incidentally some of Government House at the same time. One of the undeniably good things about the British rule is that it left behind one of the finest selection of administrative buildings one could possibly have. In fact, the whole of New Delhi is lovely, wide streets, with a wide grassy verge and trees on either side, roundabouts, cycle tracks, and a magnificent shopping centre, on a circle a mile in circumference, with very English shops. Down Parliament Street you come first to the Council Chamber, a completely circular building with a round, domed building within. At the end of the road are the two blocks of the Secretariat, with Government House through wide gardens on the right, and between the two a monument topped by the solid six-pointed Star of India. Life-size statues of King Edward and Queen Alexandra face you on opposite sides of the broad flight of steps leading into the main hall of Government House. The vast, circular hall is pillared and domed, and has the most wonderful glass chandelier. The exhibition went right back to the days of the Indus civilisation and shows carving, sculpture, painting, weaving and textiles etc. Very interesting but I am afraid I was more taken with the high-pillared halls and the chandeliers which shone like cascades and clusters of diamonds.

I walked back to the Jantar Mantar. This is a most weird-looking place. It was built in the 12th century by Jai Singh who had a bent towards mathematics. Its maths were regrettably mostly beyond me. There were two structures resembling open gasometers used to find the altitude and azimuth of the sun, an outsize sundial and two tipped-up semicircles for determining declination of the sun.

12 TUESDAY

Today I went exploring with Mavis, an Indian girl on holiday from the hills.

We went to Firozabad. I ought to explain that there were 7 cities built from time to time in the neighbourhood of the present city, all in the Jumna Valley and in a 5-mile radius. If I tell you their names then you will be able to refer to them when we come to them.

1) Old Delhi (the real old one, as opposed to the present city which is called Old Delhi to differentiate it from the new) where the old

Hindu city was, built by the slave dynasty. Chiefly important for the Kutb Minar.

2) Siri

built by Ala-ud-din in 1303

only the walls are left

3) Tughlaqabad

built by the first Emperor of the Tughlaq line in 1327

ruins and a tomb

4) Jahanpanah

built by Mohammed Shan in 1327

connecting up 1) and 2)

5) Firozabad

built by Firoz in 1354

very near the present city

6) Purana Qila

built by Humayun and Shere Shahin 1540-45

near New Delhi and sometimes called the old fort.

7) Shahjahanabad

built by him in 1638-58

the present Old Delhi with the Red Fort and the Jami 'Masjid

It seems almost impossible to get in to the Jami Masjid, as most of the time it is closed. Around Firozabad are the ruins of a wall which enclosed the town. Inside is what would be a lovely garden if it were not for the fact that in all directions are refugees from partition still living in tents   here. There are only two buildings remaining, one a high platform on the top of which is fixed one of Ashoka's pillars. He was a king who lived B.C. and was the first man to make stone buildings. He amused himself by having laws carved on stone pillars and stuck up all over the place. Nearby are the ruins of a mosque. The architecture is solid and very uninspiring.

We took a tonga along to the Purana Qila. The walls are in ruins but the gates are intact. The chief place of interest is the octagonal library. It is on the first floor up a very steep flight of steps down which Humayun is supposed to have fallen to his death. Our next visit was to Humayun's tomb and here the scenes are disgusting. The marble dome and decorated platform on which it stands indicate an interesting view close-up but refugees are in every nook and cranny and even inside the actual tomb itself. The dirt and filth are indescribable and one would have thought that even Hindus would have some consideration for Muslim sanctuaries, but unfortunately they have none.

WEDNESDAY JANUARY 12

Mavis and I cycled to New Delhi this morning to
meet Pamela, the sister of some of the children
I taught last year. By the way, cycling in
India is something quite unique - admittedly,
London and Cambridge are pretty hair-raising
centres, but that is nothing to here where you
have to cope with buses and cars that think
they own the road and no one else should be
there; bullock carts which have a sideways
as well as a forwards motion, and out of the
centre of whose wheels there is invariably a
sharp iron spike sticking, presumably to wound
any cyclist who comes too near; tongas which
go backwards at times as well as forwards and
sideways; herds of cows and buffaloes who stroll
along the road singly or together, regardless
of anyone; pack mules that jog along with loads
projecting far out on either side; occasional
goats and chickens that rush out without any
warning; pedestrians who do not know the first
rudiments of the Highway Code and probably
care even less, in addition to which they are
apparently all stone deaf and cross the road in
blind faith; other cyclists intent, apparently,
on getting themselves killed as quickly as
possible; cycle rickshaws which usually have

raucous hooters or bells. There are no rules of the road, and the procedure for turning sharply to the right is to put out your left hand, wait until someone has almost overtaken you and then swerve straight across the road. However, if your nerves are good and you keep awake, cycling can be one of the quickest means of transport. We went around Connaught Place, the shopping centre and then down Queensway to see Memorial Arch, the Indian 'Arc de Triomphe', carved on which are the names of every Indian soldier who died in the 1914-18 war. Beyond is a statue of King George V. Both are surrounded on all sides by parkland and the roadway to Government House is lined on either side with lakes. If you stand with your back to the statue of George, you can look through the Arch straight along between the north and south blocks of the Secretariat to the Star of India Monument bisecting the dome of Government House. We visited the Kashmir Arts Emporium, a lovely place with lovely things at lovely prices. I had a real indulgence at teatime when we went to the Alps cafe with Swiss pictures all round the walls. To the accompaniment of a dance band we drank coffee and ate chicken deluxe sandwiches (3 layers of bread with chicken, tomato and chutney in between on a plate decorated with potato crisps and salted peanuts), cream cornets and a milkshake.

SATURDAY

I managed to cycle down the Chandni Chowk, one of the most crowded bazars in Delhi, which I consider quite an achievement. Later, I went up on the ridge and cycled along it past the great blocks of red sandstone, the colourful bushes and the shrubs, to the Mutiny Memorial. From the top one looked out onto the town on three sides, disappearing into the usual heat haze. The ridge wound back along the other, rather like the New Forest scenery. I had a tremendous rush in the afternoon to get heaps of things done and finally set off to visit the Kutb Minar at 3.15. Trees grew alongside the road to start with I passed Wellington Airport and out into the open country, sandy and uneven with ruins scattered about and the inevitable refugees. Gaunt tombs stood silhouetted against the sun, and signposts told you what everything was: the walls of Siri over on the left and the palaces and the mosques of Jahanpanah I passed without going in. I saw the tower of the Kutb Minar when I was at least 5 miles away and it was not long before I was there. Old

Delhi is quite unique, as far as I have seen
so far. The Quwwat-ul-Islam mosque has square-
shaped arches with carved pillars orangy-brown
in colour. In the centre of the mosque stands
an iron pillar about whose origin there is
much speculation. It is thought to have been
built 1,600 years ago and is one solid piece
of iron carved at the top. The Kutb Minar
itself was probably a pillar of victory and
part of a mosque, too – it is a most wonderful
sight with its strong circular base, 5 storeys
high, getting narrower towards the top, and is
238 feet high and this is even more wonderful
when you remember that it was built 700 years
ago. Of course I climbed up to the top 100-
-200--300--75 steps round and round and you
certainly seem to be on top of the world when
you get to the top-miles and miles of plains
all round, people the size of doll's house
dwellers below. I was told that only 6 or 7
people could get on the top together, but there
were at least 20 when I was there. I managed
to get back to New Delhi in the daylight, but
I had to cycle home from there in the dark.
None of the bicycles here have lights, so it
did not matter that I did not have any either.
By law you are supposed to, but no one ever
bothers, not even the policemen! Occasionally

when they have nothing better to do the police haul in a few offenders and fine them, but they would never catch everybody, so normally they just don't bother. I managed to get along quite quickly and avoid bumping into other cycles and bullock carts and being bumped into by cars.

MONDAY JANUARY 17

I arrived at Ludhiana at 5 a.m. after a very comfortable journey in a second-class compartment for Inter Class fare. There were a few interruptions such as a howling baby, a wheel which sang a mournful song every time we slowed down and started off, and a rattly window. There were 3 women and 6 men in the compartment and I had half a berth.

MONDAY – THURSDAY

I am having a lovely rest here. What with breakfast in bed, reading, typing, meeting people, playing tennis and badminton with the American missionaries next door. Ludhiana Bazar is just as much fun as all the others – only narrower in parts. We cycled there and at one point I found that my bicycle would not move and looking down saw that someone's foot was caught underneath it. All is quiet now in Ludhiana, but just after Independence there was the most dreadful rioting and the hospital of the Women's Christian Medical College became a relief centre. They used to go out to the temporary camps, cope with inoculating everyone, look after the wounded etc., always wondering what was going to happen next, even crossing the road between college and hospital under armed guard. Apparently friends and relations used to call on the wounded in hospital, Sikhs bringing with them their knives and four-foot-long swords. Feelings being rather high and the atmosphere tense, it was decided that this was not very safe and so a 'sword park' was instituted outside the wards where visitors were requested to leave their weapons.

The compound here is big and there are 150 girls in training to be doctors and others training to be nurses. The Punjab have now asked them to stay open and increase the standard of their examinations and they will also be coeducational in the future, too. There are lab staff quarters, a students' hostel, a nurses' home, administrative buildings and the rambling hospital on the other side of the road, which they are hoping to rebuild soon if funds are forthcoming. It all started in 1894 with 4 rooms, 4 wards, 2 missionary doctors and 4 students.

Kutb Mosque -
Old Delhi

Tomb - Old Delhi

Kutb Minar

Demonstration -
Chowringhee, Calcutta
(Netaji's Birthday)

FRIDAY JANUARY 21

I managed to find a nice second-class compartment last night, once more on Inter Class fare and had a whole berth to myself. At first there were no other females there at all, but this morning a whole family got in. It is a glorious morning, although cold, and once more we are speeding over the plains seeing all the usual sights. There are plenty of monkeys about and also some beautiful peacocks. We passed through Lucknow at 1.30 and Benares at 6.30. Though it was very dark, as we went over the Ganges Bridge one could see the lights reflecting in the water and the moon rising in clouds over a distant temple. I slept well despite an invasion of people at 1.30 a.m. who made a dreadful lot of noise – apparently the rule in India is to make as much noise as one possibly can, particularly late at night or early in the morning.

SATURDAY

We arrived at Howrah about 1.30 and amidst a welter of people I managed to get a taxi to the Corletts.

After a very welcome and extremely necessary and bath, I had some lunch and went to tea with Tony and his cousin Johnnie (by tram),

for what would have cost 2/- by taxi! Andrew came round after tea and took me for a trip round the Midan (like Hyde Park on a bigger scale) on the back of his motorbike (Tony and

Andrew are two friends that I made on the boat).

SUNDAY

After the service and a lesson in playing the organ, I went to lunch with Andrew and his friend Leif, a Danish boy. There was a mile-long procession of about 200,000 people down the road (Chowringhee) celebrating Netaji's birthday. He has something to do with the Indian National Army, I think. Having viewed this from the vantage point of the roof and then consumed $\frac{1}{2}$ a lb of Cadbury's Milk Tray, we went for another ride on the motorbike and then to tea with Tony. I took Andrew and Henry off to church with me (Henry is one of Tony's friends). The church was packed and what with Andrew singing loudly and very much out of tune on one side of me, and Henry singing slightly out of tune and deafeningly loudly on the other side of me, and me in the middle trying to drown them both, I was almost a nervous wreck by the end of the service. It was grand seeing some of the old boys and girls again. Those who only left 6 weeks ago are already longing to see the hills again.

MONDAY

I had a very busy morning doing various bits of shopping etc. At 1 p.m. I met Henry to have lunch with him – that meant going round the New Market to buy it first. That was very amusing. Shopping in India is very unlike shopping at home. All the shops of one sort are close together (for instance, you get onions at one place, potatoes at another and tomatoes at another etc.) That means you sample anything edible like cheese at three or four shops before you decide which you are going to buy, walk away from one shop and pretend to go to another so that they will put the price down a bit. It takes a long time, but is great fun, and you get quite a good feed on the way. By the time it was cooked we did not get our dinner till 4.20 p.m.

Denis (one of the boys here last year) came to see me off and at 6.30 we arrived at Sealdah and had the Customs to cope with. Unfortunately, the railway to Kalimpong goes through Pakistan, and they are afraid you may drop off bales of cloth etc. On your way through they search your luggage beforehand. The Inter Class Customs are merely a mad medley of people with one Customs officer to deal with it all. I managed quite well, although you need your eyes about you all the time or things would be pinched. I found an Inter Zenana almost empty and with Denis who had nobly run around, looked after the luggage, and talked all the Hindi necessary, Andrew, who brought me some books to read, and Henry, to see me off, it was all very nice.

Its now 11 p.m. and all is well, apart from me shouting to people at the stations that this carriage is 'women only' and will they just take themselves off (in Hindi, of course). The train has an appallingly shrill and unmusical whistle which it uses with unfailing regularity at signals, stations and most of the rest of the time, too.

TUESDAY JANUARY 25

From 2 a.m. onwards I had the whole compartment to myself. In the morning I kept looking anxiously out of the window for a sight of the hills. When I saw them dark against the morning sky with the snows shining above them, I felt that I was almost home again. Every mile in the car up from Siliguri was one mile nearer home, for although I had had a grand holiday, it was lovely to be back in the hills again.

Six weeks and 3,000 miles on £35.

1949

SCENES FROM SCHOOL

After the holidays I returned to DGH and was asked to take over the choir and learn to play the organ, I was not great but I did my best. Boys had to pump it to make it work until we had a Hammond organ donated. A lovely English church was built in the grounds by the playing fields and this was surrounded with all the cottages the children lived in supervised by adults and fed with the help of a cook and a bearer.

Discipline was strict but life was good and many of the children who had suffered neglect gained much from the loving environment and have gone on to do well in their adult lives. I kept in touch with many of them and on my travels later in life managed to visit a great many of them all over the world.

I helped with Girl Guides and camping trips, swimming in waterfalls and the Rilli River, but no matter how hard I tried I was useless at lighting fires... Youth meetings, drama and sport continued, and many old boys and girls returned to help.

The farm supplied our food; there was a clothing department and a workshop which were always busy. Children helped with jobs: the most popular one was tying cloths to their feet and sliding around polishing floors.

I don't remember the date the earthquake happened but we were all in Jarvie Hall watching a film. Suddenly the floor shook, the lights fused and the building was swaying. Luckily there was no damage to the school buildings but many houses in the town disappeared in landslides and part of the toy train was washed away into the Teesta River where there was severe flooding. Power was not restored for a very long time.

People from all over the world came to work at DGH and visits from important people were always exciting as we would have celebrations with cakes and jellabies.

Lady Mountbatten was the school's Patroness and would arrive by helicopter in the playing fields. The King of Sweden came and a frequent visitor was Rajagopalachari who was an Indian

LADY MOUNTBATTEN'S VISIT

lawyer, writer and Independence activist. I
still had no news from Alan but was too busy
to bother much.

In September 1949 I was organising a coconut shy in the pouring rain wearing an old mac and wellingtons. Later, I was told by a friend that a visitor from Calcutta had said to his friend that I was the girl he was going to marry. I thought he was one of those "posh folk from the plains": in fact he lived only a few miles from me in London and was working in India with an engineering firm. He himself had been born in Kurseong along with his brother and six sisters; his parents taught at Victoria School in Kurseong. He was keen to see the country. He asked me out and in those days that meant going for long walks. We got on well and he returned for more visits. We both returned to UK that December as my father was ill and it was his holiday. We became engaged in the UK and I asked him to buy saris for my choir rather than a ring. The girls looked beautiful. Presents were not something I went in for!

Life went on at DGH and when I went to Calcutta for a weekend Alan appeared and tried to renew our friendship. I remember eating a Chinese meal with him, listening to his excusesfor not communicating with me for two years, and saying goodbye with no regrets.

DIARY OF A SIKKIM TREK MAY 1950

SATURDAY MAY 20TH

At 7 a.m. with the station wagon loaded with
five boxes outside and every conceivable thing
inside, from bananas to butterfly nets and from
salt bags for leeches to sacks of tomatoes, we
set off from the bazar. We were six this time
and included two men, Ron and Ray, along with
Ann who replaced Sheila, and the other three
of the previous trek. Amongst other things
we were in search of tea shops, Tibetans and
tropical flowers. We lurched gaily along the
road consuming sandwiches and crossed the
frontier into Sikkim. A very young policeman
bulging with importance decided that we were
too heavily laden but a few words from Ron
in the stentorian tones of an ex-Army major
soon quelled all objections. The next hitch

occurred when we drew up at a notice informing us that the road was closed till 12 noon as they were clearing away a landslide! However, a few words with the Sikh in charge got us through without any delay as the Sikh wanted a lift to Gangtok which we were able to give him. The wagon took us three miles out of Gangtok where to our great relief we found one mule and four horses awaiting us. The two muleteers (whom we christened Barefoot and Boots) loaded up without a murmur – or at least only a few unintelligible ones – and after consuming lunch, mostly in the road because of the proximity of the leeches, we set off on the first stage of the journey. We went half a mile uphill and then nine miles downhill which was a very pleasant way to start. We stopped at the first tea shop and then continued steadily, passing the mules because they were going so slowly, and we wandered down into a wonderful restful greenness. Trees, creepers, ferns, grass, wet and shining in the sun, were everywhere and always there was the sound of rushing water in our ears. As we descended it became hotter and more humid – not so bad going down but some members of the party were already contemplating the return! We were joined by a 'repeating' Tibetan, very happy, very drunk, and very hiccupy. When we reached the Dikchu Dak Bungalow we found two other people there, but they were very obliging – understandable since they were not supposed to be there at all – they had come over the Donkya La which is a pass about 18,000 ft high. So the kitchen was full of people, most of whom understood my feeble Hindi. After the usual cups of tea and cake which we consumed whenever we arrived anywhere, in fact on the slightest excuse whatsoever, we prepared for supper. What with packing the next day's lunch as well, together with the shortage of saucepans and the fact that I was back at my old job of 'fire-blower-upper', this took about 3 hours. We then washed in three inches of water (it all has to be carried half a mile, from the nearest waterfall) and went to bed at 8.30. We bombed the insects and settled down to sleep on mattresses on the floor. (I got so used to sleeping on the floor that when we returned to civilisation I had to transfer to the floor for several nights in order to sleep properly.) We put the two men on the verandah among the malarial mosquitoes but neither of them suffered any ill effects. We are not very well organised yet as, in spite of lists of contents, it is very difficult to remember which things go in which of the five boxes.

KINCHENJUNGA 28,150ft

From
Kalimpong

From
Singhik

Mules & horses
loaded up

Half a mile
uphill

SUNDAY

The night rain stopped about 5 a.m., and after
the party had breakfasted (two bits of fried
bread short as these went up in flames when the
cook deserted her post) and smothered their
legs in salt as a defence against leeches, we
set off less heavily laden than the previous
day. Even though it was only 7 a.m. it was
quite hot and we were thankful that the path
was shaded by trees, plants and clammy rocks
and wound gently up and down beside the muddy
Teesta River. Before long, we came upon a bridge
made of two pieces of wire for handholds,
and attached to these by fibres were lengths

of bamboo on which you put your feet. Ray
started gingerly across when a Nepali from the
other side literally rushed across with the
bridge swaying dizzily over the roaring waters
beneath and offered to carry Ray over on his
back. The offer was declined and we continued
our journey. The path led through damp, dark
forests with trees interlaced with vines and
tendrils through which the shafts of sunlight
scarcely pierced. Before long the path ascended
with a vengeance all the way to Mungan where
there was a tea shop at which we all stopped.
We chatted in sign language with a group of
Tibetans who gathered around and then a monk
took us into a Buddhist shrine where there
were holy books, bowls of water with flowers
floating on top, a pile of rice, charm boxes
and bits of coloured paper, all of which are
part of the puja or worship – and lovely scented
wood from the nearby forests was burning. The
increase in altitude, together with the added
strength given by the cups of tea, hastened
our steps to Singhik, a beautiful bungalow
famous for its view, unfortunately hidden in
mist. Here we found all the mules and horses
had arrived and fires were alight and before
long, we had heated cans of water and we all
had hot baths. Ray discovered and removed a

caterpillar and a large specimen of Tibetan louse from his person. We had our usual tea and cakes and, after a rest, supper was organised. The chowkidar and Barefoot blew up the fires and we had a good meal in spite of an abundance of salt in the leeks and white sauce made in the frying pan. There is a shortage of cutlery, too, and you can only have one out of a knife, fork or spoon.

During our walk today we crossed a suspension bridge 250 ft long and 300 feet above the Rang Rang River which flows through a gorge carved out of solid rock. The hills around here are very steep, too, and it looks as if someone has taken a knife and slashed great V-shapes on the hillsides to which the trees cling for dear life.

MONDAY

This was a nice quiet day, pouring with rain nearly all the time. So the main occupations were reading, eating and sleeping, with a few short walks to keep muscles loosened up. We heard some lovely birds - blackbirds, castanet birds, G.I. birds (whose call resembled an American wolf whistle) and birds which just laughed at us - and who could blame them?!

TUESDAY

It rained all night and since I was sleeping on the verandah I made myself leech-proof with a magic line of salt all round the mattress. The rain showed no sign of abating so we left, clad in a variety of macs and headgear, at 7.30. By 9.30 the rain had stopped. It was a lovely walk on a rambling path always among the greenness of the trees with the sound and the sight of the muddy Teesta River far below and with waterfalls tinkling down beside us. We made pretty good speed and did not dare to stop as there were a whole army of leeches on the lookout for juicy legs. The salt was very useful, even though we found ourselves giving half of it away to leechy Tibetans. The path wound down past a most magnificent waterfall with three branches at the top where a steamy a load of water fell and paused and fell into space, thundering downwards in opaque whiteness. Through green woodland, cliffs of grey rock, over stepping stones, so we went onwards along a pathway scattered with ducks, dogs, sheep and cows until we passed Toong Dak Bungalow and dropped steeply down to the suspension bridge over the river. In the old days they used to fling criminals from this bridge, the idea being that if they were innocent, then they would survive - there seemed little hope of that in the dirty, swirling, tumultuous torrent sweeping down the valley. There was a dank, sulphurous, decayed smell in this part of the valley and this followed us as we trod the path, often having to make detours to avoid recent landslides. I asked three successive Tibetans the distance to Chungthang and always received the same reply - 3 miles. However, eventually we got there and found the bungalow · on an area of flat land at the confluence of the Lachung and Lachen rivers. The Lachung is the clean one and that is the way we are going tomorrow. We are hoping the weather will clear up and meanwhile we have the cheering prospect of a comfortable bungalow, hot water, a fire to dry our clothes, and a large supper. Ron retired to bed with a cold, a hot-water bottle and a drink of brandy and lemon. We shall all write letters by candlelight as we have discovered that the weekly post leaves tomorrow.

The Nepali on the bamboo bridge

The waterfall

Suspension Bridge

Tibetan tea-shop

WEDNESDAY

The day started with the loss of one of the
horses - at least that was the story they told
us - but we have the feeling that they probably
(sorry, typing a bit odd) lent it to a pal of
theirs! Anyway with a great deal of grumbling
we eventually got them off at 8 a.m. with
Barefoot carrying the bread on his back. They
wanted to leave part of the luggage behind but
we would not let them. We soon passed the mules
and walked along the valley with the usual
detours to avoid landslides. First the road
led through a forest and then opened out into
a wider valley and wandered in and out over
a cultivated area between stone walls which
marked the boundaries of the fields of wheat
and barley. Houses with two storeys - animals
below and people above - stood in their own
piece of ground and children ran along beside
us shouting continuously and unavailingly
for 'baksheesh'. Up and up went the road,
round waterfalls, over stony grassland, thro
woodlands with red rhododendron trees until
at last we could look down onto the roof of
the bungalow. We descended happily, consuming
wild strawberries and followed by a cheerful
Tibetan boy who was quite dumb (literally).

The cantilever bridge

Ray

Ron & Ruby
Sikkimese
children

Ron and Ruby arrived last as they had consumed salted Tibetan tea on the way. Lachung School greeted our approach with loud noise and we sat on the steps of the bungalow to wait for the mules. There were apple trees all around us, the grey boulders of the riverbed, huge rocks brought down in times of floods; ahead, the busties of the village on the other side, the roofs of the houses being held on with rocks. Beyond were grassy slopes rising to tree-clad crags with bare patches of rock and ice-filled niches, and above it all white clouds floated in the sky. Behind us was a wonderful waterfall cascading from a crack in a sheer wall of rock. The local policeman helped us to light the fire pending the arrival of the chowkidar, and 2 hours later some of the mules came: however, the bread, one horse and one muleteer are still missing, but with tea, strawberries, condensed milk inside us and a blazing fire to sit by we are quite content. It is 8,600 ft above sea level here and the bungalow has double windows to combat the winter cold.

THURSDAY

At 7 a.m. the bread and the muleteer did turn up but there is no sign of the missing horse. At

last after a lot more arguing they got started
with the baggage and we followed. As usual it
was raining when we started but it soon cleared
up and for part of the way we were walking in
brilliant sunshine. First the road led through
apple orchards and then through forests ablaze
with all shades of rhododendrons, red, yellow,
mauve, pink, orange, the ground carpeted with
yellow and mauve violets, primulas and other
wild flowers. The track wound up a narrow gorge
with the river cascading beside us in masses
of white and green and there were glorious
views of snow-clad peaks through the shifting
mists of the distance. Next the road meandered
over moorland and there was no sign of leeches
which made a pleasant change. There were larch
and fir trees, rhododendrons, grey and white
boulders and springy grass. We met a weather-
beaten chap who had just crossed the SebuLa and
DonkyaLa (passes). The mules went slowly past
us while we were having lunch and afterwards
we rounded a corner to find that one of the
horses had slipped off the path and fallen in
the stream. The loads were in the water and,
as some of these contained bedding, we removed
them from the horse as quickly as possible.
Then by dint of much heaving and tugging on
mane and tail we managed to get the poor horse

onto its four feet again. It refused to go very far and, although Barefoot returned to it after we reached the bungalow and was supposed to give it brandy and sugar, the poor creature died. So now we have only three horses, and one of these is suffering from poisoning through eating rhododendron leaves.

YUMTHANG

Yaks

Lachung River

Ruby, Betty, Ray, myself, Ann
and the chowkidar

Yumthang Bungalow is a very nice one with a delightfully ancient chowkidar. To the east were forest-clad slopes with snow and glaciers above, while in the west the snow came right down low among the crevices in the mountains. The mist swirled down so we couldn't see very much and all night long it teemed with rain, but we were comfortable in warm beds by blazing fires.

FRIDAY

It rained practically all day. Other folk came to the bungalow and it was necessary to 'bag' a few of the saucepans and keep them in a place of safety. Ron went off to have a bath in the hot springs, the others went off to find a glacier and I wandered by myself along the path towards the Donkya Ia. (We couldn't go over it as there are no more dak bungalows this way and we had no camping equipment.) I got tired of the flat path wandering through forests of trees covered with dead moss rather like Snow White's nightmare wood, so for a bit of variety I nipped up the side of a waterfall. We were already at over 13,500 feet and I had a vague idea of climbing to over 14,150 feet so that I could exceed the height climbed on the previous trek! I started miniature landslides as I went and as the slope was almost perpendicular I soon sat down and looked at the river far below meandering on a bed of shingle and the wooded, cloud-covered slope beyond. There are lovely blue poppies up here and some little blue birds with orange fantails and others with red on their wings and tails. Having climbed up on all fours I now slid down, bringing part of the mountain with me. It then started to pour with

Sunrise at Yumthang

rain and I returned to the bungalow meeting the
others who had not found the glacier but only
a mule and yak track. In the evening Ann and I

walked up behind the bungalow to the snow line and Ann found yellow spurge, mauve primulas, white stitchwort, pink viburnum, blue poppies (the words are hers, not mine!) We brought back some of the snow to wipe Ray's fevered brow. Ron still has altitude head but his cold is better. The Nepali servants of the other people here are extremely helpful - they wash pots, fetch the water, etc. and tonight one of them made us a very nice fish pulao. To sleep now - in hopes of a fine day tomorrow for a change.

SATURDAY

We got up at 4.30 a.m. to the sight of the snows and the promise of fine weather. It has been quite a day. To begin with, the horses were actually ready at 6 a.m. and together with the horse they had hired they were off before 7. The company then split up: Ron and Ray to wander to Lachung at their leisure, Betty and Ruby to view the glacier, Ann and I to search for her missing watch and to try and climb to 14,200 ft.

We had awoken to see a most wonderful sight. The whole valley was clear and to the east the sun rose behind the snow-clad peaks and glaciers. To the north the road to the Donkya La wound towards the snowy mountains; to the west were the gaunt, bare slopes, their summits lit by sunlight and white snow clinging to the cracks in the hills. Out ran Ron like a schoolboy waving his cine camera and shouting, 'It's wonderful!' Out ran Ray in his silk pyjamas, though he quickly retreated owing to the icy quality of the air. In the fields below us the yaks were grazing placidly on the summer pastures – yaks with white heads and tails as well as the ordinary black ones.

After breakfast we all set off. Ann and I climbed through slippery, sloshy, dead forest, with moss-covered branches, searching for the watch. We came out onto a slope covered with pink and yellow rhododendrons (I wonder why the pastel shades are the only ones at these altitudes) and then walked past dead, bare tree trunks stripped of their leaves by the frost. We went on up to open, windswept moorland with snow peaks all around us and the valleys far below. One felt quite literally on top of the world and completely alone in it. It was icy-cold and we both had headaches so we mutually decided that we had reached 14,200 ft (though one wondered subsequently if one really had) and casting regretful glances at the 15,500-ft measured peak in front of us, we slithered down again. On the way Ann gave a shout of joy as she discovered her watch lying on a rock just waiting to be found.

The mountain air and the quick descent made us feel slightly tipsy so we followed the example of the river and meandered back to the Bungalow. At 11 a.m. we set off for the hot springs, passing the dead horse on the way. We crossed the cantilever bridge and went up to the small building housing the sulphur springs. There was a four-foot-square hole into which hot water smelling of sulphur poured from a crack in the rocks, and it was a very pleasant way of washing as the hot water was just the right temperature to be comfortably warm. Afterwards we had a cup of hot tea with yaks' milk in it. This was provided by a Tibetan woman living in the nearby busti. Then we carried on with renewed energy, although it seemed a very long way to the Lachung bungalow (we had to return the same way).

When we arrived we found that Ruby had taken over the cooking for the evening so we were able to go up to see the waterfall. An argument ensued as to whether the brown, plate-like growths were stalactites or fungi, but it was

On top of the world
(over 14,000ft)

Rhododendrons

The road to the
hot springs

The cook !!

impossible to get near enough to the rocks to find out. After supper the fun started. First Ray upset a kettle of boiling water all over his ankles, and then Ron fell through his chair. When Ron had picked himself up and Ray had been given first aid, we heard the sound of drums, cymbals and trumpets coming nearer and nearer; it was a most eerie sound in the darkness. Then who should arrive but the Dewan (ruler) of Sikkim and his entourage. He was complete with a horse and an Oxford accent and was a very pleasant young man. He allowed us to stay on at the Bungalow, although constitutionally he had every right to throw us out. He sat and drank tea and chatted to us while his bodyguard stood by the door doubtless bringing some fleas and lice into the place! Chungthang Bungalow is occupied by the rest of his party so we shall have to go on to Toong tomorrow.

SUNDAY MAY 28TH

We got up at 4.30 to a nice, fine day. I cooked the breakfast in the midst of the Diwan's servants. As usual there was trouble about the horses. Barefoot had hired two coolies to carry the extra luggage and when asked for a riding mule that Ray could have he said he

could get one for Rs 12. It turned out that
he intended to give us our own block mule
without either saddle or bridle. Roy decided
that he could walk (you must excuse the typing
from here onwards as the A key has broken off
completely!!) I typed o's for a's and then
inked them in.

We set out with the wind in our faces, the sun
shining, the birds singing and the waterfall
roaring a farewell. The Diwan was sitting on
the verandah in an ancient suit and a tweed
hat. At Chungthang we found that the road we
had previously come along was under water and
we had to proceed on a zigzag course on banks
between flooded fields. The Chungthang Bung was
deserted and all the furniture had been moved
as the chowkidar was afraid the river would
change course and wash away the bungalow. The
river is undermining the foundations of the
bridge but we crossed safely, noting only the
normal swaying motion. We sat and watched all
the baggage safely across and set off on the
last lap. At Chungthang we felt fine but by
the time we had made all the numerous detours
necessary up and down beside the turbulent
waters with the thunder of rocks transported
by the seething currents ringing in our ears,
we were longing to see the next suspension

bridge. This bridge was subsequently washed away but we had a short rest there before the final ascent to Toong. This proved to be a delightfully small place with a nice view and some pretty birds. Ann and I slept on in the verandah — we have so many bites now that a few more won't matter. I did some experimental cooking but the chocolate and nut soufflé did not set so we drank it as a cocktail.

Negotiating Landslides

MONDAY

More excitement – Ron nearly passed out!

We set off in brilliant sunshine through a shimmering world – water sparkled, mica glinted in the rocks, bright leaves swung on the trees – it was really glorious. The eight miles to Singhik was just long enough after our double march of the day before. Ann and I arrived at 11 a.m. and proceeded to write out a posh menu to try to disguise the fact that our rations were a little meagre. All the others soon came, but Ron arrived with a Nepali escort, suffering from a terrible backache and having gone dizzy and passed out in a shallow stream where he had lain for an hour with leeches crawling over him. We put him to bed and spent the rest of the day lazily.

The menu gives some idea of what we ate on treks. Everything had to be taken with us and very little tinned food was available in India. The milk was powdered and the bread was by now a mass of mould which has to be cut off, leaving a small, edible centre.

Lunch

Singhik salad

Corned beef or cheese

Ginger nuts

Tea

Tea

Sikkim pancakes

Toast bahut chhota (very small)

Jam

Biscuits

Tea

Supper

Dhal soup à la Kanchenjunga (i.e. plus veg)

Vista Fish Palau

Beans deluxe à la fromage (we are fed up with these runner beans now)

Steamed honey pudding à la beehive

(This boiled too quickly and was renamed honey fudge)

The Locals

Sunrise over Kinchenjunga at Singhile

TUESDAY

From my dreams in which gold watches, muleteers
and Calcutta were inextricably mixed, I was
awoken at 3.50 a.m. by a prod on the toe and
ahead of me (for we were on the verandah
again) was the most marvellous sight I have
ever seen. The whole Kanchenjunga range was
visible, shining white in the moonlight with
a deep blue sky beyond. Slowly the sky grew
lighter until it had an orangy tinge and then
the golden rays of the sun touched the top
of Kanchenjunga and the eastward-facing slope
become suffused with pink light while an area
stood out sharply as the dividing line between
light and darkness. Then the sunlight crept

down over the other peaks and the sky turned
back to a delicate blue with a trail of little,
fluffy orange clouds following each other over
the summits as if a train had just passed.
Then the snows regained their whiteness and
the light grew in strength. Everyone came out
and took photographs, the one yellow filter
going the rounds. Many people have come here
to see such a view and been disappointed time
after time, so we felt we were very fortunate.
The mountains seemed so near that one wants to
climb one before breakfast.

After a meal and with the mules well ahead,
and Ron, too, we set off for Dikchu with our
legs once again well salted against leeches. We
found messages from Ron scratched at intervals
along the path – 'So far, so good. I'll be in
Mungan before you.' And there we caught up
with him, waiting for us in the tea shop. It
was interesting crossing the waterfalls and
noting how some of them had cut deep gashes
across the grain of the rocks while others
went with the grain and left smooth slabs. We
saw many more birds, red and green ones, some
of the laughing ones, and one we called the
clock-winder-up. We arrived at Dikchu at 1
o'clock very hot, and continued to sweat till
the late evening. We hoped to have the place

to ourselves but a female Mexican Buddhist
arrived, having just crossed the Donkya La in
three feet of snow. Later a Finnish missionary
swelled the gathering. The road ahead of us is
down in several places and today is the first
time that mules have been able to get through
for a week. It seems a pity to be going back to
civilisation again.

WEDNESDAY

I did not write this part till much later so my
impressions are a little hazy. We rose early
and had a substantial breakfast using up all
the oddments. The main memory is of a long,
steady uphill plod which went on and on and on
with only two tea shops to rest in. However,
we got there in the end and, over the top of
the hill where the motor road began, we found
the station wagon waiting for us. We settled
with the muleteers and loaded up and were soon
rolling homewards singing all the songs in our
repertoire. Back in Kalimpong by 3.30 at the
end of another grand trek.

Another Tea shop

Homeward - all of us will Barefoot and Boots and
The station wagon driver

Back to Kalimpong Bazar

1950

Wedding 1950

Eddy and I did not want a fuss so got married in Calcutta at the Old Mission Church with a special licence in June 1950. The temperature was 105 degrees with 100% humidity, so I was surprised how good the wedding picture was. We went to church in the same car, had a cup of tea with the vicar and a meal at the Grand Hotel. I remember dancing the polka with Eddy but he was a much better dancer than me. I was very happy and content.

The India I will always remember was full of life and death. Wedding processions winding through the dusty streets: a garlanded groom on a white horse with bands drumming to clear his path on his way to fetch his bride. She would also be elaborately decorated with expensive jewellery and henna tattoos. My wedding by comparison was very dull but it suited both of us, the money better spent on other things.

Sorrow was also felt, through the same streets, groups carrying a shrouded body on a wooden frame, draped in white cloths and heaped with jasmine, roses, marigolds and perfumed oils, on their way to the burning ghats. Here by a river the dead are cremated on funeral pyres of sandalwood and scented logs, their grief for all to see.

I remember thinking that if I was still in

India when I died, that would be a perfect way to say goodbye, but maybe I would have to have been a Hindu??

India is the most fascinating and equally frustrating place to live. Dealing with bureaucracy is interminable but it gives everyone a job, a female trying to buy train tickets isn't possible in some areas, the caste system is dreadful, the list is endless but its beauty and majesty and the people make it a wonderful place to be for me.

1951-1956

What a change it was living in Calcutta after the peace of the hills. Eddy had a ground-floor flat on Ballygunge Circular Road which was considered a suitable area for expats and was near to the cricket ground where he played every week along with hockey and tennis. He had a cook, a bearer and a sweeper with his job as an engineer. I wanted to do my own cooking and shopping but as Michael was nearly due I accepted the situation. Apart from the heat, life was pretty easy, walking with the pram to the cricket ground, meeting friends for meals and Carey Baptist Church was a large part of our lives.

Eddy taught me to drive here amid the cows, bullock carts, people, cars, buses and tuk tuks, but I passed my test without bribing anyone. I caught paratyphoid and ended up in hospital at some point.

I started to do my own shopping until I realised the chickens were bought live and I had to kill them myself, so that soon stopped. Lessons in Hindi helped me to talk and write quite well but Bengali was too hard. I was DGH social worker and visited some very difficult poor areas to find children who needed sponsoring and found that quite difficult to see so much poverty.

Trisha was born, Michael went to nursery school and, 18 months later, Richard came along. All born in the East India Clinic in Calcutta, dedicated at Carey Baptist Church. Masses of paperwork had to be produced for them all to be registered as British citizens of the UK and Colonies by the High Commissioner in India.

Eddy then decided he wanted to work in DGH but the job was for a PE teacher so we sailed back to UK and he enrolled on a six-month course in Loughborough while I caught up with family and friends.

1956

We returned to India with Eddy's new qualifications to teach at DGH – three weeks on a ship and two days on a train with three small children and crates of luggage. Memories are vague thankfully as it can't have been easy. It was good to be back in Kalimpong, living in Fraser Cottage for the next two years, with 18 senior boys, thankfully with a cook and a bearer to help us to look after them. Eddy ran the workshop and taught PE so was very popular, and I was back as geography teacher in the senior school, so all was well. Susan was born in September. Our children had a wild, bohemian lifestyle and soon were running around without shoes like the Indian children and racing off with the older boys and girls into the surrounding hills on ponies and catching butterflies, and the school swimming pool where they all learnt to swim very early on (survival maybe?). I was frowned upon as I would not have an ayah (nanny) for the children, I realise now it would have given a job to a local lady but at the time I wanted to care for them myself.

We played tennis and the Prime Minister of Bhutan and the Dalai Lama's brother were often joining in the tournaments.

Eddy's trip 1957

Eddy went off on a trip to Sandakphu 12,000
ft up in the Himalayas.

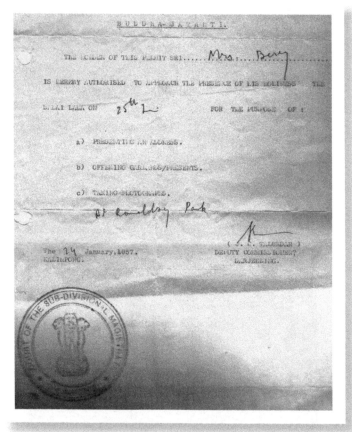

1957 Dalai Lama

In 1957 the 14th Dalai Lama Tenzin Gyatso visited DGH to speak to his many followers using our sports field which was the only large, flat area on Deolo Hill, having been dug out some years before by hand. The pavilion was painted saffron for his visit. He was a very pleasant young man of 23 and Eddy and I had personal printed invitations to be in his presence, which we still have as it was so special. Given the turmoil created by the Chinese invasion of Tibet in 1950 the Indian PM had to give his promise that he would ensure that the Dalai Lama would return to Tibet, which he did at that point. However, what we didn't realise at the time was that in March 1959 he slipped away in disguise with his entourage, from Norbulingka in Lhasa, and escaped on foot over the treacherous Himalayas on an epic, 15-day journey, ending up in Tawang Monastery in India and being granted "more than asylum, he was an honoured guest".

Strong security was put in place to prevent his kidnap and he was to be moved away from Kalimpong which was a controversial border area. We were all thrilled with this news, having spoken with him two years earlier. He has never been back to Tibet and remains in exile in Dharamsala in India, as the spiritual leader of the Tibetan people. This was headline news around the world so we were later interviewed in 1959, back in the UK, by a local newspaper because someone told them that we had met the Dalai Lama. Our family picture was in the paper.

Birmingham Evening Mail

APRIL 1959

We had a lot to learn still and had to punish
boys for stealing maize cobs from the farm,

but mostly they entertained themselves playing marbles and flying kites, along with doing chores and learning to live in a community. Eddy became Treasurer so we moved into Wolseley House in 1958, but he became quite ill so we felt it best to return to England.

So in January 1959 we had to leave. I was heartbroken: had we had more patience and dealt with the matter more wisely, then we may still have been for many more years as the principal was eventually asked to leave, and the older staff who had more wisdom survived there for many more years.

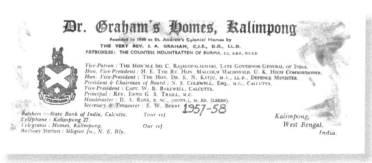

Dr G's Homes Kalimpong

We left our home and travelled many miles across India on trains with four small children who were eight, six, four and two, with 17 crates of luggage to Cochin in Kerala, South India. We returned on an Italian boat sailing

to Italy, then caught trains to Paris and
Calais and a ferry to Dover. Eddy had to dash
down the railway track in Madras to find our
luggage, and three of the children got shut on
the ledge between the porthole and the cabin
in Sicily during afternoon naps: luckily there
were wooden slats so they were not asphyxiated.
The train from Milan was full so we laid the
children on the floor of a first-class carriage
and refused to move!!

Words almost fail to describe that journey
but the Lord looked after us as always and
there was plenty to laugh about later.

We arrived safely eventually in the UK and
the next phase of our lives began.

1960-1990

The next 30 years passed in Birmingham with Eddy
and me teaching in local schools, immersing
ourselves at Shirley Baptist Church then other
local churches, organising Youth Hostel trips
with pupils and family: the most memorable were
abroad to Switzerland, Germany and Norway. I
managed to learn enough of each language to be
useful. In the UK we hiked a lot. In the Lake
District, Hadrian's Wall, the Cleveland Way,
Offa's Dyke and then the Pennine Way for Shelter,

a homeless charity, and raised £700. In those days this was a lot of money. With the family nearly all our holidays were in Youth Hostels, being the cheapest way of taking four children away in school holidays. We conquered all the highest mountains we could find, including Ben Nevis, Snowdon and Helvellyn. I organised The Duke of Edinburgh awards and had many trips to Buckingham Palace when the girls obtained the Gold Awards. Eddy eventually went when Trisha got her Gold in 1968; their car broke down and when the police saw the invitation from The Duke of Edinburgh they had a police escort!!

The children grew up, two going on to university; one joined the tax office and one became a nurse. Then there were three weddings, and eventually Eddy and I retired early in 1979.

Six grandchildren arrived between 1978 and 1982. My mother, who had lived with us for many years, died in 1980 aged 97. Eddy had not been well and had a triple bypass in 1984 and recovered fairly well. Eddy and I used to take the grandchildren away in school holidays to the Forest of Dean and Lee Bay in Devon. As teachers we would help them learn, read and act out a book and had fun with *Lorna Doone* and *The Lion, the Witch and the Wardrobe* as highlights. We would return them to their respective parents exhausted, with a bag of dirty, smelly clothes, a few plasters and bandages on various parts of their bodies, but with enormous smiles on their faces ready for the next adventure.

Holidays with Grandchildren

I had many trips during this time, with Eddy to Ireland and Scotland, or with my sister or with church groups to Israel to meet friends and study. Our church then began to support Christian church groups in Romania: unable to visit the country at this time, we couldn't go across the border until after Ceauşescu and his wife were deposed and sentenced to death by execution in December 1989 for genocide. We then loaded up minibuses, taking supplies many times, and friends still support them to this day.

South Africa to visit Eddy's sister was troubling for me as apartheid was still in force, and only abolished in 1991. Then I went to Malawi, Zimbabwe and other parts of Africa to visit Bible groups I supported.

I also had a calling to go to China as a Bible courier. I was told to be careful of what I said and who I told. My children had guessed it was not a holiday because of my involvement with the suffering churches, and helped me pack a sports bag with Bibles, which I could hardly carry! Many millions there were asking for Bibles as a revival was going on but suppressed by the government, and if discovered, people suffered persecution and death. I did not know the group I was travelling with; we were based in Hong Kong and made three or four trips a week into South China, leaving our parcels in designated places, never meeting the Christians there. I went knowing the Lord would protect me. Spiritually and mentally it was a challenging time but knowing we were supported by prayer was comforting.

Even my passport containing so many travel stamps from some of the countries I had visited potentially was a problem, but all was well and I was not arrested and imprisoned as some folk expected, as the Lord looked after me. I have to say I was happy to return safely to my family.

India was still in my heart to return at some point.

DECEMBER 24 1976

We had friends to tea, prepared the turkey and watched films. Richard (nicknamed Bez) went off drinking somewhere with his pals. At 11.45pm, on his way home, he stepped into the road and was badly injured. We arrived at the Accident Hospital intensive care and only I was allowed to see him. He was not expected to survive and the pain was so terrible he wanted to die. We thanked God there were no injuries to his head or brain or spine, but he needed 41 pints of blood transfusions (which he tried to pay back over the years). Then his kidneys failed and while on dialysis his broken leg could not be operated on, blood poisoning set in and his left leg had to be amputated. His survival was a miracle and he was able to use crutches once he was discharged six months later, 4 stone lighter, and he learnt to walk again.

He was very positive, eventually, mostly because it was his fault so he had no one to blame.

This was a difficult and emotional journey for him and the rest of the family, and I am including two of his poems as they are an important part of my life story and reflect honestly his trauma, healing and recovery.

PHILOSOPHISING ON REFLECTION

When it happens you wonder why
My God loves me this I know
Those words come flooding back
Into the memory, from the recesses of
the past
My God loves me. Does He??
Nothing can be said to relieve the hurt
So why is it that inner peace survives
such a terrible blow

Why don't I think of, why don't I
ponder on
What is gone, lost for ever
Such a large chunk of ones daily
existence
One's way of life is removed.
Yet such physical things pale into
insignificance
In the general view of life
Other things, different things
Things never before considered
Become important.
Life has enough variety to support this
Enough to make continued existence
worthwhile.

14/07/1977 Richard Berry

I LIVE TO LOVE AND LOVE TO LIVE

One day whole and normal
The next unknowing, bent, broken
damaged for ever
Never to be again the same
The numbness, the sensation of
emptiness
Helplessness, remorse.
He wondering, the questions that come
to mind

Because you just don't know what will
happen
What will it all be like?
These words weigh uppermost and then
all are answered
One word
FAITH
Describes it all.
Especially other people's faith
transmitted through prayers
Their prayers, your own prayers.
Ours is not to reason why
Who can see any good
Any evidence of God's love
And yet, still, purpose and meaning
remain in one's life

17/07/1977 Richard Berry

Richard went back to work, later got married
in 1991 and gave us two more grandchildren,
and later he and his family became Christians,
which was one of the greatest joys of my life.

At the end of 1987 Richard said he wanted to
go to India with me to see where he was born.

1988

We left Gatwick on Feb. 15th 1988 with Emirate airways who ignored our excess luggage and gave us 6-course meals and limitless free drink! So we relaxed in luxury. We stopped off in Dubai in more luxury. My handwritten diary for the trip has archway signs at the side representing doorways which the Lord gave us as the text I had before I went was: "I will make doorways for you". (Whether these are to sleep under or go through remains to be seen.) Bez bought some Scotch whiskey to keep for 'contingencies'! We arrived in Delhi at 0600 and walked straight through Customs with all our gifts, only being asked, "Have you got a video camera?" which we hadn't. We waited for an hour before our friends came, as they thought we would be held up at Customs.

After breakfast and unpacking the gifts for this family, including the toys sent by Helen and Daniel for the children, Bez sat on the balcony and said, "More has happened on this road in the last half-hour than happens in Telford for a month." My old school friend, Maggie, came to see us. She is unhappy about many things, particularly that the Darjeeling area has a 40-day bund (like a general strike) called by the GNLF (Ghurkaland National Liberation Force) and we ought not to go there. (But this might be the only time Bez was able to come to India and I wanted him to see where he lived for his first few years.)

We had a good journey to Calcutta (as it was spelt then) in the Rajdhani Express train with food and bedding provided free. Bez gave his lower bunk to a mother and her 2 children and hopped up to the top one. We all slept well and awoke to Indian music, tea and biscuits, other passengers either sleeping or meditating in lotus positions, while wide-awake India outside had hundreds of people walking along the railway lines to work.

We were greeted by Rose and Wai who feared they would be late as the car had a puncture and the spare wheel had been stolen so they had to come in a taxi. Their flat was full of Sam's (Wai's brother) family so we unpacked more presents and celebrated our safe arrival.

With Richard, India 1988

In Calcutta with Rose

India 1988

The temperature was 85 F and 80% humidity. Wai took us out to get Indian money and Bez photographed the maze of electricity wires hanging everywhere and the church where Eddy and I got married. We drove to the cricket club and past the flat where we lived and Michael nearly fell to his death by climbing on the balcony rail. We also went to the nursing home where Bez was born and found that one of the doctors there knew the surgeon in Birmingham who had amputated his leg!

The next day, I had an apt text from Isaiah 45:2: "I will go before you and unwind the snarls". A lot of them were looming. We needed permits to go to Assam and to Meghalaya and to Darjeeling, from 3 different buildings; the news contained accounts of landmines, arson, oil embargoes and earthquakes in those areas.

We went into the Carey church compound to see the children at the Day Care Centre. Rose and Wai run Samaritans Help of India, which is a charity helping poor children in various parts of NE India to have somewhere to do their homework, have a good meal and learn about the love of Jesus for them. Rose and Wai live in the centre of Calcutta and help a lot of other people, too, run holiday Bible Clubs, Bible studies, visit the other areas where there are DCCs and have people to stay and to meet and provide transport. I have known Rose for many years (met in 1949) and she has coped with illness (right up to 2005 when I am writing this) and continues to rejoice in the Lord and find daily strength from Him, as does Wai. They are a wonderful example to us all. In the afternoon we went to the New Market to find sandals for Bez but ended up in Chowringhee (one of the main roads) and got Rs 65 reduced to 20. Bez gave the spare one to a beggar boy who sold it back to the seller for Rs 2. Meanwhile, Bez had realised the immunity of pedestrians (car drivers are liable to be lynched if they hit one) and so he stood in the middle of the road snapping oncoming traffic, Lucas 'King of the road' lights (he worked for Lucas), and an Orson Welles advert and a Royal Enfield motorbike. I went to an evening Bible study while Bez looked for beer but it was yet another dry day! After a wonderful meal at an Indian restaurant we came home to climb over sleeping bodies on the floor in the entrance and up the 49 steps to bed.

Next day one of the "doors" was opened and we got the Meghalaya permit with no trouble, but Assam was tough so we went to the British Embassy to protest but they said they could not help. We found a shop selling beer so that cheered us up, and the following day we got the Assam permit, possibly because I was a teacher and the lady wanted a letter to recommend her daughter for a local school. Then we tackled, for the second time, Writers Building, where most employees were either sleeping, drinking cups of tea or looking at piles of files, to get a permit for nature reserves in the foothills of the Himalayas. This was granted plus a permit for Darjeeling, although they did not think we would get there! We returned by foot, as people were hanging out of the trams, to a party for the children at the DCC where I spoke and gave presents – I only brought enough for 20, but there were 38 there and somehow there was enough for all.

We had repacked with as little as possible because we knew we would probably have to carry it all ourselves up in the hills. On the evening of the 20th of February we set off for Sealdah station which now has a flyover and no refugees but is still as chaotic as ever inside. We shared a compartment with 2 Mr. Boses, who shared their curry and chapatis with us. We slept well and when we woke the scenery was exactly the same and Bez refused to believe there were any mountains. We had to go to the Foreign Visitors' Registration Office and they said, "You can't go to Darjeeling or Kurseong. There's a bund." But God opened a door again and we got a cycle rickshaw to Siliguri and found a taxi that was willing to take us up the back way! Soon Bez believed the mountains were there as we went up some of the slopes in 1st gear. We reached Kurseong and had a letter to stay from Sam to a friend who lived 3 miles beyond the town. No one would take us in case they got shot, but I believe God sent an angel, because a white car appeared and took us there. Mrs. Sinha (Akomummy) was thrilled to see us and gave us the best bedroom, boiled some water to drink, heated bathwater and apologised for the fact that there was little food, but we shared the sandwiches we had been given in Calcutta, and she cooked rice and dhal and vegetables out of the garden. She was sad and scared so it was lovely to be able to encourage her and hear about her family in Shillong. I went up to see Father Abraham's community project of egg production, cows and pigs plus 40 orphans and a school of 1,700. He came from Canada 40 years ago and is a Catholic priest who believes in teaching local people to work better on their own land and educate children to live in their own environment. At present he is feeling depressed as he sees a life's work being ruined by all the present troubles – also he is upset because 2 days ago one of the orphan boys was shot dead when he ran away from the police in fear. The banks are closed so he cannot get any money and will have to pay his workers with eggs! Everyone is living on eggs because of the bund on transport out of the area. Bez went to see him and gave him the bottle of whiskey (a fair contingency) and a packet of cigarettes, for which he was very grateful.

The beauty of the hills is all around and yet there is all this sadness brought about by misunderstanding, greed, misplaced enthusiasm and political manipulators. The GNLF do not wish to be under West Bengal but to have their own hill council. It is a reasonable request because Britain made one state without considering the wide differences between people of the plains and those of the hills.

In the house where we are you feel as if time had stood still and it pours with rain at intervals, which is not cheering as we shall have to do a lot of hitch-hiking! Normally this road resounds to the sound of horns, changing gears and hooting toy trains. However, 2 buses passed last night with a police escort. Most people were amazed to see how brave we were to have come but I felt God was allowing it so we had no need to be bothered.

The next day, Bez and I went towards Kurseong to see the school where his father was born and told Akomummy we would get her some food. We only had to walk one mile before an Army lorry stopped for us and 12 soldiers with rifles saw us on our way. We went to the bazar and bought bread, rice, dhal, bananas and apples. We found a taxi willing to take us up the 1,500 ft to Victoria and Dow Hill schools. The taxi could only get up the steep slopes by keeping his foot on the 1st gear! The schools were deserted of course, but the chowkidars showed us round and we took lots of photos in dull weather. Everywhere looked run-down, tatty and in need of repair. Eddy's parents worked here and 5 of their 8 children were born nearby. His brother was killed in the Battle of Britain and we saw his name on the honours list. When we got back (in a taxi) we watched the TV news and found there had been 4 killed, 3 wounded and 55 arrested near Kurseong last night. There is an air of depression among hotel owners who are going bankrupt and shop owners with no customers. The roads are bad and landslides have not been cleared.

For Feb. 23rd the text for the day was very apt — FAINT NOT — for we were hitching to Darjeeling. Life here is very different from simple, moving slowly and you feel so much love. We carried our bags over our backs and walked steadily uphill by the railway line. Bez is followed by crowds of children wherever he goes because of his one leg. Manga had said, "The only way you will get to Darj. is in an ambulance." So we hoped to hitch in one, but they were all full of people who had been injured the previous night! We had rests for restoring circulation in Bez's hands and mouthfuls of water. The weather was now sunny and pleasant. "What a great day," I said. "We're good targets for snipers," responded Bez. "I can think of better ways of spending a morning." But after nearly 2 hours a car with a Red Cross on its windscreen stopped: the occupants squashed up and gave us a lift all the way to Darjeeling (a favourite saying in India is 'there's always room for one more').

We came into Darjeeling in a hailstorm which seemed apt in view of the decrepitude of everything and walked vertically upward to the frontier police where no one else was waiting. "Can we have a pass to Kalimpong?" The policeman replied, "Find someone to take you, then you can." We continued the uphill walk to the Bellevue Hotel where we had booked, but it was closed and the door was charred where a petrol bomb had exploded. However, for some strange reason the Tourist Office was open and they phoned the hotel who opened their door. We were given the best room (no one else was there), overlooking Kanchenjunga, which was wreathed in cloud. We had headaches from the thin air, so Bez drank beer and I drank tea and we ate biscuits. Everyone is short of food so we pretended we had had lunch. Our room was so luxurious and there was a boiler with hot water for baths. We were told not to worry if we heard bombs going off in the night.

We went for a walk up Observatory Hill but could not see any views because there are so many trees. It is sacred to Hindus, Tibetans and Chinese and there is a plethora of prayer flags, chortans, statues of Kali, Shiva and Humayun and a lot of monkeys. The rhododendrons and magnolias were magnificent. All the shops closed at 5pm and there was a voluntary curfew after dark as no one wanted to be shot. We returned to a Tibetan New Year party with lots of officials there, so we got up-to-date information. We established that it was impossible to get to Kalimpong because the GNLF have cut down the trees and stretched them over the road for a kilometre. Also there is no water or electricity because the pipelines are being used to make guns and the power station has been blown up. The busti areas around the Kalimpong Homes are hotbeds of trouble and there are bombs every day. 3 girls were kidnapped because they tried to go to work, but were subsequently released after the police had killed 6 militants. So we shall spend 2 nights here and then go in a bus convoy to Siliguri. The police were amazed at our walk here. They are in sympathy with the aims of the GNLF but not the violence. Bez said,

"I am surprised anyone drinks here because if you stumble you could fall down thousands of feet." 1st policeman: "But you can sway on the winding roads." 2nd one: "We are all short so we fall easily!" We travelled light to get here so we feel the cold but at least we have hot water and hot-water bottles. The lights are very dim so we went to bed.

One bomb went off in the night – and we heard that the arts and crafts works had been gutted. Bez said, "Giving this place self-rule would be as sensible as getting an alcoholic to run a pub. And telling the W. Bengal government to run it is like the French telling the English how to play cricket!" Our text for the day was from Acts 16:10: when the Spirit would not allow to Paul go where he wanted to – as we were not allowed to go to Kalimpong – one can have a shut doorway. We did see some of the snows so at least Bez knows they are there. We had porridge, chapatis and jam for breakfast and then went to get one film developed but it was not very successful (I think the printer had not worked for some time!). The only bright and shining place in Darjeeling was Tensing's Himalayan Mountaineering Institute, which was very interesting and our names were the first in the visitors' book since the bund started.

Even the coffee shop was bund but the children were happy collecting rhododendron flowers and climbing trees. I walked down to the Tibetan Refugee Centre 500 ft below, where 650 people lived now, to get a Tibetan outfit and order a doll for Lucy. There was no electricity for some hours back at the hotel but there was hot water, a large supper and a hot fire. I praised the Lord for our lovely warm beds.

On Feb. 25th I woke at 0530 but it was still cloudy but at 0830 we saw Kanchenjunga for one minute! I wrote more letters and as this was the day we hoped to get down to Siliguri I promised to post some for Mr. Lawang, too. We walked down for 30 minutes to 8 buses and took up 3 seats (as we are larger than the average Indian) but the tickets are only 80p each. We sat for 2 hours when all the buses revved up and then stopped again. After half an hour they went 1 km and then stopped again! Here were long arguments because the police escort had suffered damage and would not go with us. In the end 6 buses went and ours was one of them. They went very fast which could have been alarming as there were incredible curves, innumerable landslides & damaged roads with large holes gaping into space. At 1530 we arrived amid the noise and chaos of Siliguri, which was quite traumatic after 5 days of peace.

There was no room to stay at the Marina Hotel as it was full of students who could not get back to the hills, but Mr. Lawang, the owner, let us sleep in the lounge. He was a lovely Christian and asked me to lead prayers for him and five of his grandchildren. They all sang in perfect English and beautiful harmony: "All over the world the Spirit is moving..."

I promised to send him a Bible in the new version. We slept well and the plane took off on time from Bagdogra. We had our reward when it flew above the clouds and we saw the Himalayas, 28,000 ft plus, in full view. Sam met us in Guwahati and 8 of us piled into the car – which had problems, first with the dynamo, which was sorted out in a tatty garage, and later the bonnet flew up, got dented and had to be tied down with my camera strap! It was a long, hot but beautiful drive on winding roads, through forests, up to 5,000 ft. There were hundreds of tinsel-tassled lorries, rickety and overloaded and often beside the road or in it with broken axles and shedloads. No one bothers to move them: they pay the police Rs 20 a day and can do what they like, so we are told. There was a massive traffic jam in Shillong but we were home by 2pm in a lovely wooden house below the hospital on a hill.

We went off to the Day Care Centre (DCC) at the Doulos Bible Institute; the children are fed by Tearfund. 40 children were sitting at desks and greeted us with: "Good afternoon, madam and sir." They sang in perfect English songs like 'Allellujah, Jesus is coming soon' and I was asked to speak before they ate rice, dhal, egg and vegetables. Then we went to Martha and Mary's House where 23 orphans are looked after by Mrs. Plessibon - helpers come and go but find it too tough. Each girl has a small cardboard box with all her possessions. They all ran away from Richard at first, but then they crept back and sang to him. By now it was getting dark so Bok and Democracy, 2 of the workers, asked if we would like to see Shillong at night. We said Yes and then followed an incredible hour and a half negotiating the lorries queued up waiting to pass through the town after 1800 hrs and then we drove 1,000 ft upwards to the viewpoint from where a plateau of lights could be seen. We returned to a family evening with a good meal and hot baths. I slept in a room with 4 others, I had one bed and the 4 shared the other one. When the missionaries first came to Kurseong they found the ancient religion of the Khasis was one involving worshipping one god and using blood sacrifices, so on this basis it was easy to preach the Gospel. Many became Christians and there are churches of many denominations, as well as people who follow the old beliefs or none, or have brought in Hinduism or other religions.

Meghalaya has political troubles, too, and there have not been any schools open for a long time and they have curfews at night. The next day we had a fantastic journey to Cherrapunji and noted the ways people helped each other with the farming. Cherrapunji is the wettest place on earth but at this time of year it is very dry and there was only a trickle of water in the falls at Mawsmai. We met the mother of one of the boys I taught in Kalimpong. She was a small lady and made us a lovely lunch. Bez was followed by children wherever he went. We went to look over into the valley of the Brahmaputra and Bangladesh.

On the Sunday I took the children's meeting and then we set off for the game park at Kaziranga. Bok was driving a borrowed car and we had a five-and-a-half-hour journey over some bad roads because they had been washed away in last year's floods and had not yet been repaired. We stayed in a forest lodge, with air conditioning; which was not working, lights partially working and cockroaches in the sink but no mosquitoes! We were woken at 4am and off to the elephants at 5. Bez left his crutches in the taxi and climbed up the steps. Our elephant was 32 years old. In the next hour of our silent clomp we saw one horned rhinos, buffaloes, hogs, deer and a wild elephant who trumpeted at us. No tigers or leopards appeared and we gathered that a lot of animals were drowned in last year's floods. After Bez had hopped down, Bok went off to fetch the taxi, but another came back and we were informed that the driver had gone for a cup of tea and had got lost. So the crutches were locked inside and Bez had to hop to breakfast. Afterwards we went for a ride round the nature reserve as Bez now had his crutches back. It was very peaceful and we felt engulfed by peace. I think the ranger had a variation for all visitors of, "A tiger crossed this road yesterday...if you came later there would be chance of seeing a tiger..." Rhinos are still poached for their one horn, which weighs 2 kgs and sells for 15,000 Rs to be used for an aphrodisiac.

We left the tangible peace and set forth with our super driver. It was a 7-hour journey as we diverted to go over the new 3 km bridge over the Brahmaputra – a mere stream at present but 3 km wide during the monsoon. The journey to Kaziranga and back was 700 km (440 mls). We passed villages bright with bougainvilleas and the flame-of-the-forest. The signs MAN AT WORK usually meant 1 man with 20 watching. The bridge has a long approach so it is 5 and a half km long altogether. On the way home there was the astonishing sight of a man repairing a puncture in his bike sitting in the middle of the road in the dark, using the beams of oncoming cars as they swerved to avoid him. We were home by 20.00.

On March 1st I walked up to Manga's house at 0600 to have fellowship with her followed by breakfast. Storms came and went but I walked back in sunshine. Bez discovered it was a dry day yet again because of wages being paid. The next day's schedule seemed impossible but all was accomplished.

Walked to Ward Park at 6am
Breakfast at Bok's
Saw Lahun's mother.
Collect Sam's photos
See Sam and Manga's clinics
Collect Dan's uniform
See site of new house and lay boundary stones.
Visit 2 more families.

Pack, bath, lunch.

Off to airport at 1400.

The legend about Ward's Lake is that the governor's daughter lost her ring when feeding the fish so the lake was drained and all the fish cut up until the ring was found! Bez got his beer at the golf club. When we reached the airport the conversation went like this:

"I have not got your names on my list."

"We checked them in Calcutta."

"They have not told me."

"We need the luggage or we will miss the train."

"There might not be a seat on the plane, and you can't take that luggage."

So we went for a walk and had a cup of coffee and I prayed for another doorway to open. When we returned the security man said, "You CAN take that luggage," and the airways man said, "There ARE seats."

It was great to be back in Calcutta again. It was a holiday for the Holi Puja, so the children were playing cricket in the street. In the evening Wai drove us to Howrah Station but there was a major traffic jam on Howrah Bridge so Wai told us to get out and walk and said he would find a coolie. So our luggage was hoisted into a basket and the 4 of us set out at a brisk pace (Rose came with us). However, there was a people jam at the other end so we missed the train by 5 minutes. Bez sat on the platform with the luggage and comforted a distraught Italian girl who had also missed the train and watched a ding-dong battle in the unreserved compartments of a nearby train where bodies were flying in all directions. Meanwhile, Rose led me to the stationmasters' office as all the cancellation windows were besieged! I explained the predicament and waited nearly 2 hrs while 2 seats were sorted out on the Rajdhani Express for the next day. Then Rose went to look for Wai while I was assaulted, verbally, by a station employee for allowing Partition in 1947! He gave me a book by his brother showing how India could advance if everyone helped each other. True for the whole world! At 2100 we all met each other, got to the car and spent the next 2 hours getting back over Howrah Bridge!

A new bridge was started 17 years ago but was still not finished (note in 2005 - it is open now). We only took a minimum of clothes as we were going on to Agra to see Maggie in Simla so we ended up being very cold after the heat of the plains. When we reached Delhi we got a taxi to Tluanga's - they were relieved to see us, but not worrying as they know India. By 1700 that evening we had reached the hotel in Agra. I took Bez off in a rickshaw to see the Taj by moonlight but it was closed because of the danger from Sikh militants. One of the police took us to a high part so we could look down on the Taj.

There were hordes of mosquitoes trying to get through the windows into our room but we slept peacefully.

At 0630 the rickshaw arrived and we joined other tourists. Bez was impressed and took photos, also of a family crossing the stagnant Jumna River by foot and risking decimation of same by poisonous contents of water. The place is not cared for as it used to be.

After breakfast we booked a taxi to Fatehpur Sikri, Red Fort, Itmud-Ud-Daula, which I have written about during previous trip. After much searching, Bez found an open wine shop and drank 2 bottles of beer on the station and in the loo. We got back to Delhi for the night.

I narrowly missed being hit by a newspaper on the verandah at 0600 as these are delivered direct from bicycles! I spent most of Sunday at various services at churches and spoke at Sunday schools to the children. We caught the night train to Kalka and slept well, catching the toy train at 0600 the next morning. We only saw Simla in rain and clouds. It was a lovely trip up winding through the mountains - 919 curves, 102 tunnels, 845 bridges, 19 stations, speed 25kph max., max. gradients 3%, distance 95.5 km, from 65m to 2,075m (7,000 ft). It was pouring with rain at Summerhill but Maggie and her driver met us, greatly relieved as our phone message was garbled and she did not know how we would arrive. It was now 1230 so we obviously had to stay the night. Maggie was organised for us. She showed us over the viceregal lodge - an astonishing affair - like an English stately home. There were teak carved walls inside, thick carpets, preserved bedrooms and antique furniture. It is now used for 25 advanced study personnel - no wonder there is some jealousy of Maggie's position as Principal. She gave us a piano recital after supper. We had a roaring fire and comfortable beds.

After breakfast Bez read while Maggie and I had a good natter. She was touched that we had taken the trouble to come and see her for 12 hours, even though it worked out longer! It is great travelling with Richard as he never grumbles and accepts all that happens with NO PROBLEM, I LOVE IT or THEY ARE QUITE MAD. I went for a walk but came back in a hailstorm with a leaking umbrella. We went to the bus stop by car and had a comfortable wind down to

Chandigarh, wrapped in tea cloths!

That town was like Milton Keynes. It was specially built as the combined capital of Punjab and Haryana, but not accepted by either! In 10 minutes we were off in a deluxe bus with a video in a cacophony of continuous hooters and high-pitched singing, plus a Hindi film. Anyway it was comfortable and fast and only took 9 hrs against 14 hrs by train. So we were at Tluanga's by 2300. The next day, our last in India, we hoped to go shopping but everywhere was shut because of the bund, except the gift emporium where we spent our last Rs 2,000 and Bez bought an assortment of Indian cigarettes for presents! We encountered the two and a half lakhs of people marching on Raj Bhavan (250,000). There were plenty of police around but all was peaceful. "This is just like the Gandhi film," said Bez. Then we found a taxi and went to Qutb Minar, India Gate, Connaught Circus, Raj Ghat, Nehru's House, Jantar Mantar and Mizoram House. Home to supper and a bath and we slept till 2 a.m. Off to the airport in a taxi and the nightwatchman waved farewell. It was an easy flight home, to be met by Michael and then to see Eddy and the family.

The end of a wonderful holiday. Praise the Lord.

After this trip Richard became unwell and
both kidneys failed. So he was on dialysis for
a while waiting for a kidney transplant which
he got eventually thankfully.

INDIA 1995

God gave me: "I will teach you in the way you should go. I will watch over you and satisfy your needs."

This will be a summary of a summary, as my first attempt disappeared.

I am into the trip to India in Dec 1995. First to Calcutta via Amman and an evening meeting in Chinatown to lead, followed by a plane to Guwahati and car to Shillong to help in a VBS (holiday Bible Club) with 158 children meeting in a Hindu school. I had the seniors and showed a video after numerous problems solved by poking bare electric wires into the sockets and securing with matches! Sundays were non-stop from 0800 to 1900 with sermons and Sunday schools, drums and guitars accompanied the singing and everyone prayed out loud together in various languages. Every car ride is a miracle of survival; no one has driving tests, traffic jams are endemic, and the standard joke is: "Want a lift in my car?" "No thanks, I am in a hurry." I found 2 of the 3 Khasi students I took to Wales in 1991. The ground we put the boundary stones round in '88 now has a house big enough for all the family. Manga's house has been enlarged and there is a flat on the roof where I stayed

Every time I had a few days back in Cal. I helped the DCC (Day Care Centre) children, led Bible studies, preached, visited and prayed with folk. It was a really blessed time. Cal. has around 15 million people in it in the daytime and you need to look up and sideways as well as down in case you collide with doors, drainpipes etc, or fall down a hole or trip over an ancient typewriter where a letter is being tapped out for one of the illiterates. You can also fall over someone asleep on the pavement.

I went on a 4-hour train journey to Jamshedpur where Cyril runs some DCCs and also built a Bible college (doors and windows are added as the money comes in.) We managed to get a ticket for the train back by pushing into the 2nd-class queue (as women are allowed to do) and then jogging along the platform to get to our seats as Indian trains are very long and usually leave on time.

At the end of January I went to Mizoram — not direct, as the plane was cancelled — so I had to go via Assam and have a 6-hour taxi ride in a jeep without doors. It was a wonder neither the live chickens nor I fell out, as the road was continuous bends. I had one day to adjust and it was Sunday and as 90% of Mizos are registered as Christians, I was whisked from one church to another. The Lord told me to speak at the teachers' meeting on 1 Timothy, so I did and it went well and was backed up by the Education Minister who arrived an hour late. I also taught the song, "Shine, Jesus, shine," to the assembly at a Catholic school as one of my Soon Bible Club leaders taught there. I was told that the Mizos were once headhunters and had attacked a tea planter so the British soldiers had hanged 2 guilty ones from the lamp-posts. "You must dislike the British," I said. "No," was the reply, "if they had not stopped us being headhunters we should have beheaded all the missionaries when they came and we should not have heard the Gospel."

I flew to Cal. and next day went on the 12-hour train journey to Siliguri and then 2 hours by bus to Kalimpong. There was a taxi strike there, but the Lord continued to watch over me and someone got me a lift to where Manga was staying. The next day we prayer-walked round the Homes and I also prayed for a thunderstorm to clear away the mist. It happened and we were able to see the snowy peaks of the Himalayas for the next 2 days.

Next we headed for Darjeeling in a borrowed jeep so I could get the carpet from the Tibetan refugee centre that Richard had ordered and paid for but not received. This was accomplished and in the course of the journey we met people who had helped him and me in 1988 - like Mr. Lawang, Akomummy, Father Abraham, and Mr. Edwards. We visited Jaigaon, on the borders of Bhutan, and saw more DCCs, delivered letters to the underground church in Bhutan, as well as speaking at churches and children's meetings. Although Bhutan is a closed country you can wander over the frontier for a few kilometres without anyone bothering. There are many problems between the Bhutanese and the Nepalese who were brought in to work for them. Deepak (now called Daniel) is one of those I got to know well and 10 years later continue to help. We returned to Siliguri and the jeep went back to Kalimpong. I went to see Mr. Edwards at the Marina Hotel and missed the plane to Delhi, but they found another seat for me on a private plane.

Tluanga (whom Eddy taught at Bible Class in Cal. many years ago) met me and we exchanged news about Mizoram. I saw my school friend, now a professor, Maggie, who is still lecturing around the world and writing books about Gandhi, February is the wedding season so the streets were often blocked with dancing guests, brass bands, horses and lorries with generators for all the lights. I saw other folk and the highlight was a Sunday service with 24 Nepalese giving their testimonies and 4 of them were from Kalimpong.

I went back to Cal by train and joined Rose in a 7-fold prayer walk round Carey Baptist Church. I had another time of prayer with Debbie Misao, as her brother was into drugs. (He is now healed – 2005 – and working with his mother in an orphanage in Manipur.)

The next day, I was off to Visakhapatnam in the south by air. And then there was a 4-hour jeep ride to Lamtaput in Orissa. Our driver was used to lorries and drove along the single-track road with all its impediments as if he was on the fast lane of the M5. This place is on a 3,000 ft plateau over the Eastern Ghats and is an area of tribal people whom Christian Indians, mainly from Kerala, have come to help by building a hospital, school and encouraging villagers to learn to read and write and to tell them about God's love for them, for most are animists. There is a farm here and great vision for future work. After 2 years the land is growing vegetables but is in need of irrigation and I said, "You need someone to come from Israel and teach you." VP, the one in charge, replied, "Why don't I go to Israel and find out." Actually this happened the next year as I had enough for his fare and the Israeli agricultural folk took him around and even sent out some helpers from their land to Lamtaput for a few weeks. The hospital is called Asha Kiran (Ray of Hope) and the school Anand Niketan (Place of Eternity).

Later there was a short 6-hour train journey to Purulia to visit a leprosy hospital, started 100 years ago and, although this disease is now curable there is still prejudice against those who have had leprosy.

I was back in Calcutta for my last few days, preaching and praying with people and being given yet more gifts to bring home. I prayed about the packing and, praise the Lord, everything went in and by carrying the heavy things in 2 small bags I got the rest into 3 cases weighing only 28 kg and was not charged excess.

There is so much more I have written but this must end as so much more happened in later years, but maybe I need advice on what to write as I have many other trips to other countries, too. After a night in a posh hotel in Amman we flew via Berlin and I arrived home on March 3rd 1996.

Eddy's bypass had lasted 12 years and he died in July 1996. We had a lovely Thanksgiving service for him and many friends from India came. I was relieved he was now with the Lord and out of pain.

Richard then became unwell again and his transplanted kidney failed, so he went back on dialysis for a few years. Eventually Michael, my eldest, donated a kidney in 1997 and this worked really well for him for 13 years. Sadly he died unexpectedly aged 56 in 2011. He had lived life to the full and was now at peace.

INDIA 1997-1998

MEGHALAYA, SHILLONG, DEC 21ST. - JAN 2ND

There is TERRORISM - in the North East - missionaries came 100 years or so ago and so there are many Christians, committed and nominal, but there are groups, mainly of the young, often led by people living in other countries, trying to get complete independence from the Central Government in India. The idea is wrong because no state could be self-sufficient but the unrest is fomented by people who want to disrupt Indian democracy, there are always justifications because bribery and corruption are safe, often among so-called Christians who have brought the name of Christ into disrepute. Shillong is in Meghalaya, which gained its separation from Asia (on the grounds their Khasi people are different) peacefully

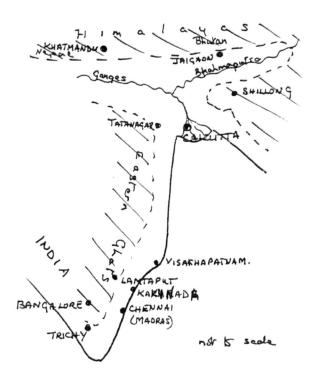

Trip by myself in 1998

and does not have much trouble but there are
groups who would like to stir up trouble, many
criminals join them and there are robberies
etc. However, the local people, despairing of
police action, form themselves into vigilante
groups when necessary. The folk near here did
this & successfully beat up the troublemakers

and a drug pusher was killed – body removed by
police next day, no questions! But in Nagaland
there are 2 opposing groups who spend the day
in prayer & fasting, praying for success in
killing the others, citing the Old Testament
for support of their actions for "justice". At
night people stay indoors and on paydays the
terrorists will be sitting at the desks taking
10% of all the wages – and, if you refuse to
give, then later you will be shot dead!

(8) CHRISTMAS IN SHILLONG
DEC 21 – JAN 2

By Dec 21st. lplanes were arriving 4 hrs late
from Delhi & I didn't want Manga, meeting me
at Suriahati, to be inconvenienced, so had
short prayer: "Lord, if possible, please lift
the fog". The plane was on time: what a thrill
to be met in the refurbished Guwahati Airport
and whisked off by Manga, with Hunlary in the
jeep. We met Shimti (nurse friend of Manga's)
at the neurological unit where there had been
tests for one of her daughters who suddenly
had headaches and a fit – she had the cyst
of a pork tapeworm in a blood vessel in her
brain. Fortunately it was discovered in time
for treatment otherwise she would have died.

We stopped halfway after coping with roads under repair or needing repair plus numerous slow-moving cars, at Nongpoh, to see Shimti's sister, Aibroster, whose house is perched up the hillside where rocks had to be blasted out of the way to make a flat surface. No lunch available as she thought we'd be later, so we ate at the Khasi cafe. Later on we stopped by the road to buy pineapples (at 5p each) papayas and vegetables (much cheaper than in the towns). As we arrived at Hunlary's house we got a puncture - convenient place - and had tea while he changed the tyre.

I hardly recognized the house on Polo Hill as it has been rebuilt and enlarged. The flat above is now complete & I had the bedroom, like a 5-star hotel, & with an electric bar fire, really appreciated, as the nights were very cold, although by 8 am the sun was up in the blue sky & I could sit on the roof and feel hot. The 3 boys all remembered me - and of course, the older ones, Richard. Yanga & Chaiwin were the same as ever and "Papa" was home.

Sam came for breakfast the next day and wanted to know what Birmingham was like these days.

Manga is beginning to feel better at last but still gets tired: her patients come to the house by 8 am and all day at her clinic and often phone in the evening. She is so caring of the babies and gives the mothers health care advice, too – like not giving 2-day-old babies mashed rice to eat! Ashish, the Buddhist boy doing his degree, who lives in one of the 4 small houses behind their house which they rent out, came to see me and ask if I could get him a job in the UK. I told him of the difficulties but will send some official documents to put him off – he thinks the Buddhists in England will look after him. In the afternoon I went to Nongmynsong with Manga to speak to the Care Groups (mostly new Christians) who meet in a small hut in a slum area – by the time we started (late as usual) people were having to sit on benches outside – it was dark before the end but they fed us on biscuits, cake and tea – about 80 of us – so full of joy and assurance of God's love. I fell off the narrow path into the field, but all was well.

The next day Samuel and Tiu with son Josiah & relative Sairos, who drove a borrowed car, came and took me out to lunch in town and then up to Shillong Peak, where 2 sightseeing families from Assam asked me to have my photo taken with them! Back to Tiu's sister, Hamapearl, for tea (she looks after Mom & Dad plus various children) and then to speak at another Care

Group meeting – at the church in town, where I know a lot of folk. Doreen, whom Richard & I met when she was 14, did the translation into Khasi – she is now studying for her PhD.

Christmas Eve was peaceful – I helped Charwin with the vegetables, packed small parcels and they decorated a "Christmas tree" (everyone here uses trees in the garden, or breaks a branch off a conifer in the forest) outside and put up the 5-pointed stars with light inside that is the main decoration of houses in Shillong. In the evening they saw the transplant video. We'd gone out for a drive in the afternoon to deliver a present to Herbert Speed (a Kalimpong boy) whose sister had sent the money from Canada via Rosemarie in London – I came out with a lot of money concealed round my waist. There were plenty of traffic jams, from last-minute shopping, plus carol singers from various churches parading the streets (as people don't go out much in the dark) and late at night there were fireworks to welcome in Christmas Day.

My gift of Roses chocolates in paper Christmas crackers was appreciated and we exchanged small presents. Yanga bought the boys a CD Visual (very expensive) We had carols from Radio Shillong for breakfast and left by jeep for the church I was preaching at, only an hour later than intended — only 1½ hrs, partly on a dirt road with the usual bumpy surface; I closed my eyes at times. It was interesting to me that the jeep was the same one Manga & I drove to Darjeeling in during 1995 as it had been sold in the church. No toilets in the village, but found a suitable rock. Terraced hillsides & forests. Church built on a hill up earth steps. I recorded some of the beautiful singing & Hunlary translated into Khasi. About 50 children and 40 adults there & I had to shake hands with all & kiss the ladies. Later we had lunch in one of the homes and drove home with Hunlary telling me about the corrupt road contractors who write out a bill for repairing a road or bridge, submit it to the Government and say it was all washed away in the monsoon, when in fact they never did any repairs at all!

After breakfast I have to climb over the 3 dogs who are very sensibly lying on the steps in the sun. On Boxing Day we went to see Mrs. Sinha, who looked after Richard & me in Kurseong in 1988 during the Gurkha Liberation Front problems. She has moved to Shillong, as her sister-in-law died, and she has bad arthritis. She lives with daughter and son-in-law (Chief Sec. to Gov. of Meghalaya) in the British Raj residency.

There are good anecdotes up here. Manga once had to go to the police station for a parking offence. "But there's no notice to say you can't park?" "We could not afford to put one up." "Then I can't afford to pay the fine." She was let off. I said to Mrs. Sinha's daughter, "Your husband has a reputation for honesty." "That's why I have to work," came the reply.

On the Sunday we had another jeep drive beyond Cherrapunji (wettest place on earth, but owing to lack of storage is short of water for 4 months in year!) to a village where their new church was being dedicated. I cut the ribbon and the Shillong Pastor, Joseph Skinner, spoke. There is a lot of revival going on in various parts of India and persecution of Christians by Hindu militants is becoming more intense. Afterwards we had a picnic in Thangkharang, a national park overlooking the plain of Bangladesh. Evans & Hulda were nearby so we had a cup of tea with then and met the family. He is accountant general in Nagaland where there is a lot of terrorism so has security guards all the time. We drove home in gathering darkness - cars don't put lights on until it's very dark, and when people are cold and have to wait, they set fire to the grass at the side of the road!

On the 28th I had lunch with Sam's family, walked over the golf course to their house and then saw daughter Susan's dental clinic in town.

I spent the 29th with Evans & Hulda, theoretically going to Jowai but never got there as Hulda called on a friend at Sohryngkham. Delightful Khasi house with silver-painted flattened kerosene tins tacked onto wooden walls (filled in with mud, straw, bamboo.) The mother was very ill, having shattered her arm in a fall and unable to move. We prayed with her. In India they say grace even before drinking a cup of tea and always pray before anyone leaves the house. We came back via Smit (see notes on Khasi religion) and had lunch at 3.30 p.m. in Shillong! Had a peaceful evening.

Soma & Pamela (he is the 3rd of the 3 young men Eddy & I met in Birmingham 1991, and remembered pruning the apple trees at 295). They all saw the transplant video. We had squid soup and momos (dumplings stuffed with meat) for supper. Very good as usual. Chickens bought live here, otherwise retailers tend to inject water into the legs etc to make them heavier!

We went past the reservoir, which supplies HEP to all the NE states, so if it ever ran dry there wouldn't be any, to Dowar Kroit (Door of the Devil) or Lover's Paradise where there are rocks by a river and the legend is that a mother put her baby on the rocks while she farmed and when she returned the rock had eaten the baby. Her tears made a poor on the rocks which is still there. We had a great picnic - all food, curry, rice etc is packed in Thermos jars so it stays hot. Jan 1st is a day when everyone goes picnicking so we went on Dec 31st instead. Came home via parks by the lake to Susan's for New Year's Eve, where I met her when she came to Cherrapunji in 1988! Then Manga & I went off to a 4-hour prayer meeting and at 11.55 pm most of Shillong let off fireworks to welcome the New Year.

Jan. 1st we went to Shimti and family, who still remember my visit in 1995 when I needed the toilet and it was only half-built. Husband is in Merchant Navy. House now completed with 4 bedrooms and is very nice. We had supper at the Hong Kong Restaurant where a meal for 7 of us cost £3 total!

On Jan 2nd, Sam drove us to Guwahati - the plane was 4 hours late but we got a free lunch and because Manju (Mrs. Sinha's daughter) came, too, we had VIP treatment and waited in armchairs in the station manager's office.

A lovely Christmas - but good to be in Calcutta again and to be warm!

(13) KHASI CULTURE & RELIGION

Khasis believe an umbilical cord came down from Heaven onto a mountain called 'Lumsopet brieng' and brought down 7 huts from which the Khasi tribe emerged. They used to be able to go up and down to Heaven to see their Creator God but because they became so sinful they were prevented. The sun was angry and refused to shine but a cock said he would sacrifice himself (blood sacrifices of animals are part of their tradition) but had no clothes. So they dressed him up & gave him a crown (hence the cockerel's bright feathers). He crowed 3 times to show the sacrifice had been accepted and then the sun shone again. If you are good you go after death to eat a betel nut with God. The moral standards are high & if you steal, say, Rs 10, they believe you will get sick and have to pay Rs 100 in hospital bills.

But a number who have become Christians still practise the old ways and use black magic against sickness and business failure.

There is a beautiful hut, made entirely of wood (wooden nails, etc) with a straw roof renewed each year where ceremonies and sacrifices of goats continue on auspicious occasions. Christians do not attend these & if a potential chief becomes a Christian he loses his position. We were able to go inside & sit on the sofas as the chief's father was there. I did not feel any "evil" in the place, I think it's mainly cultural.

You can see why it was easy to explain to Khasis about Jesus as they already had one God and the need for blood sacrifices.

(14) THE LAST TWO WEEKS IN THE NORTH EAST.

Kathmandu. Jan 6-13 Jai Masih (Christian Greeting - Victory to Jesus)

The plane flew low over the steep hills and valleys with snowcapped Himalayas towering in the background towards the orange pall of pollution which showed the position of the capital. Loknath, a Nepali relation of a friend in London, took me to UMN guest house (very comfortable and only £6 for supper, bed and breakfast compared with £60 for the same in the hotel opposite). My first impression was of a city that was like Calcutta but considerably less crowded. Clean, Westernised cafes and a lot of tourists about. I was thrilled to find Eileen Lodge, whom I knew 45 years ago in Kalimpong, was living in K. and still working

for Nepal Leprosy Mission. She was one of
the missionaries waiting, along with Nepali
evangelists, to get permission to enter Nepal.
They went in in the '50s and built a hospital in
Pokhara and the Nepali young men preached, and
often were put in prison but in 1990 freedom of
religion was granted in this Hindu kingdom and
there are thousands of Christians. Persecution
may come again as the militant Hindus, already
active in India, have a campaign to reconvert
the country.

On Thursday, when it was misty and cloudy
and very cold all day, I read and wrote and saw
Michael Chettri, whom I met in 1995 and who is
a pastor now in Hetauda, in the Terai (plains
of Nepal). At 6 am tomorrow we catch a bus for
the 9-hour journey to his town.

Needless to say, the bus was late but only
half-full as we went round the ring road past
several temples in the morning mist. At the
main bus station it filled up, the mist soon
dispersed, and we went up and over the checkpoint
– long queues waiting there but as we were a
government bus we got through easily. After
that we wound down, and then up to over 7,000
ft and down again – magnificent views of the
snows – stopped several times for "tea breaks"
– I have a useful inside which can do without

need for toilet for 10 hours! One village is called "12 loops" for obvious reasons. The steep slopes were terraced where possible for rice in summer and wheat and mustard in the winter. Cycle rickshaw to Michael's home (first floor, rented, tatty and damp in monsoons but very homely). His wife, Ganga, and 3½- & 1½-yr-old sons, Mishal & Bishal, plus her mother, uncle and various others were there. Michael hasn't spoken English for a while so I copied out my Saturday sermon (6-day week here, Sat is the day off) so he could practise. I had my first uninterrupted all-night sleep since I reached India. After cups of tea, fried egg & bread we went off to Samdan (lamp on a stand) Church nearby on the land outside the town where people have bought from the Municipality and built their own homes. They built their church a few years ago and over 100 were there. I was translated into Nepali. We ate noodles at Pastor Bishmai's home and then walked to the prayer tower. This was started 1½ years ago and they pray for 24 hrs a day every day – students, visitors, local church people. I have written about this separately as it is such an inspiring story. The church already had 5 church plants and Micheal is responsible for leadership training for CCC (Campus Crusade for

Christ) in this area of Nepal and has 7 staff.
Shyam is assistant pastor. After the service
are prayers for Tapal who has pains and bad
dreams. The healing and deliverance ministry
is very much a part of the church work here.

On Sunday morning we went back to the prayer
tower as Narayan (their leader) had asked me
to lead the Bible Study and later caught a
tempo (auto rickshaw like a van which takes 10
seated and 20 when the police are not looking)
to Ismurnak, which is a Memorial Park in memory
of Communist leaders and is being developed
as a picnic area, small zoo etc. No transport
back so walked a mile down to the road. In the
evening I sat on the treble-sized bed while the
children slept and we all watched Hindi soaps
on an old black & white TV set – no electricity
cuts today.

We left on Monday at 8 am. on a cramped,
draughty bus, on the "down" route – longer but
faster, in theory, although we had a loose bolt
underneath so had to keep stopping. So it only
took 8 hrs. Cost for each is £1! We went west
along the plains, north up a beautiful river
valley where the poor were camped on the dry
parts breaking up stones for road repairs where
the landslides from last year's monsoons had
damaged the otherwise smooth roads. Then east

as we joined the road from Kathmandu to Pokhara (where the tourists go). The only "down" part was the last few miles. We tempered through the city & I found Benjamin waiting at the guest house. I shall see him and family again in Jaigaon, but I was able to pass on the money I had brought from the Whizz & Kings Kids at our church. The bus was too late for me to book supper but Micheal took me to Royal (another Kalimpong town - etc) and we arrived at a "cottage meeting" with 3 young men from his "Friends Evangelical Church" and I was asked to lead a Bible Study (fortunately they had an English Bible - more translation into Nepali - people here are so clever; I couldn't translate into a different language). Afterwards we were given a substantial supper and walked back in the dark to Benjamin. He is worried because his little boy has ear infection and fever so we prayed for him. On Tuesday I went to see Eileen again and was glad that she was as upset about the education system as I am. It is so sad to see 3-yr-olds with satchels of books & in school uniform going to private schools and having to practise pages of letters and numbers. Mishal (3½) had "Poor" on his first report as he only got 1/20 for a Nepali exam. But "achievement" is all that matters in Nepal (and India) & no one understands about nursery schools and playing with educational toys - and if they try they are laughed at. Government schools are poor because the teachers know they will get paid, so many of them do not bother to teach. Because I have had 3 nights away from the guest house I have enough money to buy some small presents for the family, made by leprosy patients. Then I met Micheal & Benjamin for coffee and walked (not far, they said, so it took 20 minutes) to the CCC office to talk to the directors about how to send money for M & B. I was not happy as none of the methods seem foolproof, but Loknath told me to send it to his wife's sister in London and he will give it to them from his account in Nepal. I then treated them to lunch at the bakery with my remaining Rs 420! and spent a peaceful afternoon reading and writing letters. Loknath took me out to supper will his daughter Pratibha, as his wife Rosie and other daughter Vijeta are away and Pratibha does not like cooking.

I got a taxi Wednesday & had nearly enough for a cup of coffee left over after paying airport tax & the extra 3p was given me by a couple from Cardiff who are going round the world. At breakfast I met 2 young people from Vancouver state, with a sister in Vancouver and have addresses and phone nos if we want to meet them in August. Talked in Hindi at airport & had to wait as plane is delayed. I was met at Calcutta Airport by Wai as usual.

Next day I went off on the night train (air-conditioned sleeper) to Jaigaon. The most significant thing was the 18 km of devastated road leading into the town, plus the gash in the hillside where half the mountain collapsed in the monsoon, sending torrents of water and mud hurtling along destroying houses, people and roads, and flooding half the town. Having negotiated the now dust-laden main road, I met my friends at Emmanuel Baptist Church, and spoke at 4 of their meetings. I also endeavoured to lift Deepak (met in 1995 and who has written ever since) out of his state of depression, and persuade him to return to Darjeeling and get a job and stop brooding. I hope I was successful. Saw Benjamin and his family in the one room they rent - tell Joy that Ashish, the 7-yr-old son is in hospital having had 2 operations on his right ear. I had 2 more journeys on the devasted road to Chinchilla Tea Estate where there is a day centre for 50 children.

There is tension in Bhutan because some Nepalis were demonstrating as they are not allowed to live there, so I went in by jeep to deliver letters to the "underground" church (felt like a secret service agent) and to visit the Gumba Buddhist Monastery as a tourist. All successfully accomplished.

At 6 am Tuesday will be the 4th journey in a Bhutan bus to Siliguri. Another 20-minute bus ride for 6p took me to Bagdogra to the hotel where Mr. Edwards looked after Richard and me in 1988. Thrilled that Mr. Edwards was there, now 84 — in bed because of pharyngitis but mind as active as ever — plus an ex-Army nurse who looked after me. After magnificent food from his restaurant, she went to the station with me in Mr. E's car, plus driver, and put me on the crowded Darjeeling mail. Back to Calcutta again.

SUMMARY OF DOT'S INDIA VISIT 2001

There should be one for believers and one for non-believers but the nons will have to manage. Sorry. Whenever I come on a journey like this I am very conscious of the many people who are praying for me and that is the most important thing of all. Thank you. I did not imagine that these 9 weeks in India could be so wonderful, and of course the two-and-a-half week visit of Michael, my son, was the highlight.

I am sitting in Calcutta with the roar of trams, lorries, taxis, cars, scooters pounding past outside, so any conversation needs to be shouted or one has to go to the kitchen! Frequent traffic jams cause a cacophony of motor horns. My diary takes up so many pages that I am writing a few memorable events.

DELHI 13/10-26/10

Death defying rides in autorickshaws. New Delhi's wide roads and lovely parks, friendship and hospitality and being part of VPs and Ninnila's family – they insisted I use their double bed as they enjoy sleeping on the floor. Visiting an HIVIAIDS centre and seeing the children being looked after so lovingly. Driving past 100s of 1000s of cow dung and mud pats drying in the sun for fuel. The technology at the Delhi Christian Fellowship involving a laptop on the pulpit which projects choruses and notes onto the screen. Red traffic lights have RELAX written on them to reduce road rage, Temp. around 34ºC. If you want to have a party in a side street just block off the road and make the traffic divert. Anthrax scares, but none were positive, just hoaxes. Met a lot of new people, some of whom knew folk I knew! Plenty of night noise celebrating Durga Puja but much quieter Sundays than in UK. Sweated for an hour on the station till the air conditioned Rajdhani Express to Kolkata (confusing new spelling) arrived.

KOLKATA 27/10-1/11

Mike arrived at correct time. We stay next door to Wai and Rose in a lovely hotel built last year on the site of the 1992 explosion which killed 200 ! My Bombay friends are paying for it in thanks that I looked after them in Birmingham (very kind of them) and we eat with Rose and Wai. So we clamber up 4 flights of decrepit stairs daily to wonderful meals. Mike enjoyed Kol. – from visiting Carey Baptist Church where he was dedicated as a baby, to tram rides down overcrowded streets, to walks along overpopulated roads, to shopping in the New Market, travelling on the remarkably clean Metro and riding in the only hand-pulled rickshaws left in India. As well as seeing the Puja's goddesses, visiting his Dad's haunts as well as the Victoria Memorial, Indian Museum and Botanical Gardens with the 200-year-old banyan tree. He says the words "organized chaos" and "recyclable" were invented by Indians. I was amazed to find an HSBC cash point just up the road from Wai's, watched over by rifle bearing security guards.

DARJILING AND KALIMPONG 2/11-9/11

Good air trip to foot of Himalayas. Continuous twisting steep uphill drive to 5000 feet with hazards on the way. Took M. to school where Eddy was born but it was empty for Puja holidays and looked desolate. Drove on to Belle Vue Hotel in Darj. (where Richard and I stayed in '88). Owner was away with the Dalai Lama. Thick mist but the sun broke through and Mike saw the snows one morning. Walked to Tibetan Self Help Centre and bought presents. M. saw Himalayan Mountaineering Centre and the Zoo while I had a free tea at the Windemere Hotel, still reflecting the Raj of 100 years ago. Next day M. went on the ropeway and visited a tea garden as well as shopping in the Bazar, while I bought and read "A Thousand Suns" by Dominique Lapierre, which I highly recommend, although a library copy may be better as I doubt if you can buy it in UK for the 4 pounds sterling I paid in India.

Next day we went on the winding road through forests and tea gardens down to the Teesta River and up to Kalimpong, where we all lived in the '50s. M. noticed how much happier and relaxed the people are here compared to those in the plains - I think it is also to do with

Mike and me outside Windermere Hotel, Darjeeling

Outside Graham's Homes Hospital, Kalimpong

the glorious scenery you can feast your eyes
on. While he got over a headache I wandered and
sorted out an itinerary. After a misty day my
prayers were answered and the snows came out
for the next three mornings. Awe inspiring.
I danced around and praised the Lord. Mike
walked up to Deolo and I had a taxi to the
revamped top where wildness has been replaced
by a tourist hotel and viewpoints. We went
around the Homes, having tea with various folk
and Mike remembered quite a lot as he was 7
years old when we left. On Friday we went to
the other side of the hill to the Albella Homes
and saw Heshron and Dr. Ebe and left money for
the boys they look after. M. used his jumping
mouse handkerchief trick when we visited the
cottage for the small children and he also
went to the bazar, Hindu Temple and Buddhist
Monasteries, which were preparing for the Dalai
Lama's visit the day after we departed.

JAIGAON 10/11-12/11

Hired a jeep for 3 days so I could visit two
friends. Pleasant drive down the rushing river
valley and then through the Dooars tea gardens
to Benjamin's training center for evangelists
to Bhutan. Slept in basic bunks upstairs.

The five in B's family still sleeping all in one room. Great welcome. Town is full of rubbish and pollution and refugees from Bangladesh, folk from Nepal and Bengalis, latter not popular. Water has to be fetched from stand pipes (only running a few hours a day) or wells. Mike went for a walk with 2 of B's children (having been told to keep away from the river as he might be attacked (white people assumed rich)) and I prepared a talk for the 17 students. The next door Pentecostal church had a conference so there was singing and loudspeakers from 0500 to 2100! and there were Hindu Diwali celebrations at various hours too. Our driver's and the local cook's arrests by drunken policemen caused a stir but B. managed to get the fines reduced. I met Deepak whom I have written to for 6 years. He has married a Hindu and has not been going to church. Had words with him and told him he must pray she will become a Christian and meanwhile show love to her and the family (who are all Hindus) as he has been a Christian since 1983 but in a state of depression. I saw his home with Mum and sister's family, 2 rooms over the rice fields but at least he has a job and a roof and someone to be with, I gave testimony at church. M. came to the 3-hour service which

had evidence of the presence and gifts of the
Holy Spirit. Mike felt the

Holy Spirit had missed him but of
course he was not ready to receive. We
left to drive to Bagdogra at 0530 and
were able to see Mr. Edwards at the Marina
s. He was thrilled to see us. And so back to
Kolkata.

SHILLONG NOV.16TH-26TH

Meghalaya is one of the North Eastern states
written about in a book published in 1980 called
"India's North East in Flames". The flames have
died down somewhat but the problems remain. Most
were caused by the British and perpetuated by
the Central Government, who scarcely recognise
the existence of these states. Problems centre
on the 'invasion' of tribal land by people from
the plains and the inaccuracy of boundaries. The
Meghalaya Government is teetering at present.

The Khasi Students Union has accused the Chief
Minister and his cronies of being involved
in the sale of land in the Meghalaya enclave
in Kolkata in order to gain several crores
of rupees for themselves. The sale of land
has been cancelled so the buyer may sue the

government and meanwhile a committee has been set up to investigate the corruption, with the Chief Minister as Chairman!! However Manga says the Chief Minister is a devout Catholic and may have been misled.

He has initiated peace marches and days of prayer in the past. She thinks the 60% of Christians in the country should take more part in peace efforts.

On Monday I went to the Police Station to register my arrival in Shillong. Last time it took 4 people to do it, this time it was 6! There was no one in the appropriate office so I went off to find someone. Two people investigated and said the officer had gone for tea and also said something in Hindi. I then walked along a corridor labelled "No outsiders" and saw someone else who took me to another office where two more were sitting. "All I need is your rubber stamp on my passport," I said. They just looked at me. "Why does the man in charge have to go off to take his children to school?" I asked. "How do you know that?" "Because I listen and I understand Hindi," I replied.

Another man was called. Meanwhile one of them asked if I was a Christian and what denomination. So we discussed the unity there was in Jesus and how all were equal in God's sight. (I had a similar conversation with a Muslim taxi driver earlier). Then my friend, Soma, breached the "no outsiders" sign and discovered he was related to one of the men. This may have speeded things up as the 6th man reappeared waving my passport, which had been stamped, and said he was going to get it signed. I went out where I came in, and the 4 who had been waiting when I arrived and were still there, all shook my hand! It only took 20 minutes. When I went to say I was leaving, no one could be found as the office was closed and the superintendent had gone to play golf!

This is my 4th visit to Shillong as I first came here with Richard in 1988. Yanga (one of Wai's brothers) now has a very beautiful home on the top of Polo Hill and I have Manga's room instead of the flat upstairs as 2 of the sons are at college so there is plenty of room. The temperature here is 17ºC or less so I am glad of warm clothes. My knee is coping well with steep slopes and slithering in and out of shared taxis, which cost 7p for 3km! In the 10 days here I have attended the church Bez and I went to, spoken to Sunday School children about dealing with teenage years, met the Martha and Mary orphans, some of whom remember

Richard, given a one-hour sermon in a Reformed Presbyterian Church, travelled to the Union Bible College 45 minutes away on a single lane race-track type road around a reservoir and spoken to hundreds of students and addressed a teachers meeting about a holiday Bible club. The sermon was a real event as the church was full of 500 people. I have never spoken to so many all at once. Shillong is very special as I first met four of the folk I know there in Birmingham when they were studying in the '80s and '90s and took 3 of them around Wales to see where the Welsh missionaries who brought them the Gospel 100 years ago used to live! I also saw Evans and Hulda who lived by the BBI in Edgbaston. He is now the chief accountant for 3 of the NE States and has a posh government residence. Mrs Sinha who looked after Richard and me in 1988 also lives in Shillong with her daughter and family. He is secretary for all the NE States so lives in a mansion! I have invitations from all to return and hope to do so in a few years.

Apart from this I have had time to sit in the morning sun and read, as well as meeting lots of friends, including Isaac who had a 2-day bus journey from Mizoram, and Samuel Sharma and wife who came from east Bhutan. Manga is working too hard as usual as she is not only a paediatrician seeing around 50 a day but also involved in children's work at church where there are 1000 attending, and evangelism in the state of Manipur where many are embracing the Gospel.

Recently a Hindu of princely caste became a Christian after attending a meeting and then having a dream in which Jesus spoke to him. He was baptised and is now training as an evangelist. His family have vowed to kill him.

I went to Sam's (another brother of Wai) whom we stayed with in '88 and who now has a big house the other side of the golf club. I enjoyed the 2km walk there. His children are grown up and he is now a grandfather.

The highlight of my stay was when I went out to go to a 10th birthday party and was given a big hug by the driver of the rickshaw. It was Sairos who was very poorly with TB 3 years ago and to who I gave money from Kathy, my hairdresser, for medicine. He is now cured and healthy and finished schooling. He borrowed money, provided by the government, to buy the autorickshaw, and makes enough money to repay the loan, pay for his keep and help his mother in her village. She came to see me as well so I had another big hug.

Meena, another relative of Sam, took me

shopping for oddments and I went to the Butterfly Museum. It is now forbidden to catch them. The traditional Khasi New year is celebrated with music and dancing. I caught a bus to the airport at 0630 and the three and a half hour journey cost 2 pounds sterling with 4p for a cup of tea. I am not looking forward to returning to UK prices.

KOLKATA 27/11-13/12

I now sleep on a comfortable camp bed in Rose and Wai's office/sitting room. I shall miss my morning stint on the balcony at 5.45 a.m. as the lorries, taxis and buses rumble past, followed by trams, and men warm themselves round roadside fires while others wash in the ever-flowing hydrants and people buy meat from the goats who were protesting about their slaughter around 0230. The orange sun rises amid the general pollution and shines on the trees growing out of the walls opposite, where squatters continue to live in the buildings shattered by the 1992 explosion.. I have never washed my hands as much as I have here!!

I often go to the moneychanger with my passport to change dollars for Wai at an improved rate, post letters and cards at the GPO where everything (as everywhere in India) has to be

checked. Where I am staying there is a constant
stream of visitors, children are being coached in
Bengali, Hindi, Maths, reports are being written,
emails received and sent. I help where I can as
well as reading some of the innumerable books.
I thought I was going home with a lightweight
rucksack but I seem to have accumulated a lot
of gifts and presents. Fortunately one of the
parcels of books arrived in a strong GPO sack
so I have additional space! I am hoping a large
bottle of Shillong pure honey and George's
"elephant inside an elephant" will arrive intact.

I have been visited by a lot of folk. Michael
from Nepal took a day and a half to get here but
he was able to meet colleagues at the HQ of CCC
(Campus Crusade for Christ) as well as me. He is
taking a group in Nepal on an evangelistic tour
in January (I hope the Maoists have quietened
down by then). Ajit and Premila came (Leprosy
Mission) plus a converted Hindu who is cycling
round villages in Purulia giving the Gospel to the
tribal villagers, some of whom are being baptised
soon. Narayan who has prayer towers in Nepal,
had to go to Vellore in the south for his wife
to have a thyroid operation, so they, plus carer
(you have to take your own cook etc to hospitals
here) called on their way home (and invited me
to lunch with a Bengali friend from the other

side of town and I acquired a very bad case of food poisoning so have spent Tuesday and part of Wednesday being not very well.

William, from a fishing village in the south, came to collect some money given by a group of ladies in UK for his church work. I have been out with Deb Misao from Manipur, visited a Catholic Church and seen where Mother Teresa started her work, shopped in the New Market where you bargain for everything, and been to the BMS guest House for a meeting and seen the manse where Eddy, baby Mike and I lived temporarily in 1951.

I have also talked with the Gujrati Hindu girl upstairs who had a brain tumour, and bought some of her craft work, played the piano at Carey Church and led the Bible study for the eleven Singaporean students (who have been whitewashing a Bible College and sampling village life) and the 12 who normally go to the Saturday Bible class (good thing people are happy sitting on the floor in India). On Wed 12th we had the Christmas party for the remaining day care centre children that Rose and Wai look after, plus parents. Thursday evening I have the 16 hour train journey back to Delhi and will meet Tricia and Peter and then fly home after an altogether fantastic holiday .

Thank you for all your prayers.

DIARY OF DOT'S VISIT TO INDIA IN 2004

SUN 17/10 This computer is doing odd things so I will make it short. God gave me the strength to get here as at Heathrow Bus Station there were no trolleys so I had to carry all 4 bags and when I discovered a secret supply of trolleys I fell flat on my back from weight of rucksack (Mike had helpfully tied the waistband round the back to make it tidy) but was unhurt. Plane packed but good journey and was able to carry and wheel at Mumbai and be whisked off to the Soans house. Rested and back to airport at 11 p.m. More strength given and flight steward said, "You look tired. I will order a wheelchair at Kolkata." So then I travelled in style to waiting room and waited for 2 hours writing letters till Rose arrived at 0530. Kolkata is as dirty, dishevelled, rubbishy as ever at 05.00 and full of Durga puja. The roads are more potholed than ever and soon will be impassable (we had a jeep fortunately which tooted its way past everything). Talked to Rose, repacked everything so I could leave things for south of Kol. behind and slept a while, talked to visitors etc. Off to Mizoram at 1230 tomorrow. Feeling very happy. Love to all, Dot.

MON 25/10. I am leaving a week early and going to Shillong as there's not enough to do. Alexandra, a young English teacher volunteer, is here for 4 months and is 1st-class; lovely Christian and gets on with staff and children. Tluanga hoped I would share Alex's flat high up at Synod Conference Centre, , but he said I could stay in their newly completed basement with Western toilet. So carted all luggage down 4 flights (no lifts!) and then back to theirs. Slopes here are almost vertical, so houses built with cement pillars, or wooden if poor, into the rock, and vertical drops of hundreds of feet below. I got unpacked and settled, and decided to leave on 28th as daughter Zawmi was coming for a week's holiday. HOWEVER, she was coming on the 21st, plus 3 others, so I am back up at the conference centre, with so-called Western toilet (only 1/2 height) with broken seat and cracked, so bits of my bottom got stuck!! But I managed. Ate supper with Alex.

One feels very isolated up here, and Alex felt that too in August, but now knows teachers and others so can pop in for tea etc. It is a hundred and 96 steps from here to the school and ditto back, so takes me 20 minutes each way, but knee is ok. Tluanga had not worked out what I should do, and anyway it's not relevant here, as most teachers are unemployed MAs who have no teacher training, and everything is geared to mugging up and learning parrot-fashion for exams. Alex has small groups and tries to make them think for themselves and discuss, but they find it hard. I take the 15-minute prayers in the mornings and sit in on lessons, but at least I had 2 English lessons to teach, which I enjoyed. The school is on 4 floors and has no playground, so 658 children from 4 to 14 are cooped up for 5 1/2 hours each day. How do they manage?!! I have given out all the education books I brought, so at least my bag is much lighter. They have a room marked 'library', but so far it has no books. All teachers are very friendly. I asked why I could not have stayed with a family, and he said 'some Mizos are scared of white people and are afraid they might do or say something wrong.' Like most of the world, Mizoram now has drink and drug problems, and the church had a camp last weekend to help addicts get free.

It's good to have bucket baths again, boiling all the water in kettles. Tomorrow I'll be helping KG teachers to pronounce English properly! How? Just by talking with them presumably!

Tell George and Alex I used their song and dance in the school assembly today.

Tluanga offered to pay my air fares Calcutta to Aizawl to Guwahati, but I said no as I'd expected to pay myself, and to use it to encourage children who have improved. Sunrise is at 5am and very beautiful.

FRI 29/10 TO SHILLONG

Good journey – via numerous landslides as the 2 weeks of continuous rain before I arrived caused a lot of damage. Particularly to road surfaces which are never good anyway!

Apparently Kolkata was waist-deep in water at one stage. Alex touch-typed my 2 previous emails at colossal speed, so it may be worth learning to do it. Wonderful to be staying with Sam and family for a week before going to Manga's – with full-height Western toilets, hot water and luxury. Have meetings to speak at, others to attend, people to visit. Posted home unwanted schoolbooks and left friend of family attaching the 25 Rs 20 stamps with paste (nothing sticks here). Had supper out with police sergeant and family on Z alert as they are looking after the rep from Kashmir who has come for a golf match tomorrow on the reconditioned Shillong golf course. It is crossed twice by a road over which the ball is driven and if damage occurs to a car en route you get Rs 500 damages! Not sure what a person gets. We encountered someone teeing off from the road on the way home!

Everyone who remembers Richard here sends their love. Sam and Lahun hope to travel to Europe next year and get an extra day or two in London so they can see us.

TWO DAYS IN SHILLONG 13/14/11/04

I woke at 2 a.m. to go to the loo and the firecrackers were still crashing around the sky celebrating Diwali. We had a Muslim breakfast of bread dipped in soup made from cows' legs. Samuel, who was a student in Brum years ago and is now principal of the Union Bible College, picked me up in an auto rickshaw to spend the day with him and family and gave me tender cows' tongue for lunch. Then I went to see and hear the musical fountain at Ward's Lake at dusk when the spouts of water keep in time with the music (you've probably seen them in the UK). We drove back through the Diwali lights but the Kali temples were already being dismantled. Supper included fried pigs' stomach, chickens' gizzards and mushroom soup and chicken legs, including claws. We are very wasteful in UK as these internal bits are very tasty. Went to bed with exploding crackers still battering the air but by Sunday morning the church bells were ringing. I spoke to another youth group and another Sunday school, being transferred in a battered jeep which coped adequately with steep hills and narrow roads. In the latter SS I met a boy who had been in Dr Graham's Homes, Kalimpong (where we lived in the '50s). I was then taken to the free rickets clinic where Manga helps each month. Many poor children have bow-legs or knock knees from not being given enough milk or sunshine when babies, but an injection of Vit. D and proper food means it can be cured in a year. Had 2 lunches and 2 teas, one in a 120-year-old house built by British and now enlarged and using the British brass bedsteads left behind and in perfect condition. Pigs' trotters for supper!!

16/11/04 I am staying with the folk Richard

and I were with in 1988, only in a luxurious house now and am treated with so much love – plus wonderful food. I walk round the golf course every day and observe life, visit friends, speak at 8 of the 10 Sunday schools the church has (totalling 1,000 children) and to Teachers, Youth Groups and at Bible Studies. So I am very happy and feel very well. I have met Bhumen whom I have helped through college. He should get his degree on Dec. 7th. He comes from Manipur from a Hindu tribe and was converted in 1998. He is returning to Imphal to minister to his tribe, some of whom are now Christians and needs also to support his widowed mother and 4 siblings. He trusts the Lord to supply his needs so I am glad to continue to help a bit. Shillong is a lovely place, like Scotland, and ideal to live in as prices are only a quarter of those in the UK!

TEN DAYS ON THE BORDER OF BHUTAN A wonderful time in Shillong was followed by an equally wonderful one in Jaigaon. I was met at the airport by Samuel who garlanded me with marigolds (I got 7 more silk scarves from various groups later!!). We sat in a doubtful cafe by the bus station for 2 hours talking Hindi and a soldier gave me his address and wrote, "God be with you till we meet again".

The three-and-a-half-hour bus journey for Rs
63 (70p) was enlivened by a puncture and then
the worst traffic jam ever, caused by the Shatt
Hindu Puja, so we took four and a half hours!
His family greeted me with great joy and gave
me their best bedroom and all 4 piled into the
other. One is given a "programme", so my time
was filled with preaching, talking to Sunday
schools, youth groups and church meetings and
trying to sort out Daniel D (Deepak wanted a
Christian name). I met him 9 years ago and have
seen him since and written but he was still
mixed up. Main problems were caused by him
marrying a Hindu and not telling her he was
a Christian so she has run away (with money
and clothes) and his mother, who is a Hindu
of an obscure cult, blackmailing him into not
going to church because he is responsible for
her burial when she dies. However, Samuel and
I have talked to her and she likes me so I
believe she agrees that Daniel has a right to
serve his God just as she has, and he should be
getting fellowship in 2 churches now. One of
his 3 sisters is a Christian.

Jaigaon is as chaotic as ever with even more
people crowded in, whereas, just through the
gate, Bhutan is clean and peaceful and one
can visit PO, banks and internet cafes with

no queues. I have only just realised that many Bhutanese were thrown out by the King in 1992 because they voted for democracy in a referendum and he wasn't having it. Samuel's family is one of these but he was up north and was able to keep his identity card (even when he was in prison for a month for preaching the Gospel the police were sympathetic and returned it) so he can wander in and out and establish small "underground" churches. There are at least 7,000 Christians there. The Bhutanese refugees are officially recognised by the UN and have camps in Nepal, although most of the money sent for them goes into the pockets of the admin.

I am doing more walking here as the tracks are rutted and potholed and include dry riverbeds, so the auto rickshaws sway alarmingly and I refuse to ride in some! One Sunday school of 73 children was in the jungle and you should have heard them sing. I distributed cards and sweets after telling the story (from a book donated by George) and singing songs written by Alex. We walked home past the paddy fields and huts, passing a man riding a pedal bike with his 4 children on-board!!

On Tuesday I moved to Benjamin's and once more was greeted with love by his wife and 3 children and 2 dogs in their 1st-floor flat.

Benj. is helping 2 very poor areas by starting day schools as well as church and SS. In one school I spoke at, all 27 children gave me a garland or a bunch of flowers (their teachers get Rs 500 per month).

It is in a tea garden 2 hours' journey away where his family went to from Bhutan after they were told they had to work without wages. His mother lives there with one son who works for Govt so has a small house. There's another son there too with family. Benj. used to work for Govt in Thimphu for a while but left to do Christian work so had to leave Bhutan. We had a great day out driven by Raju. Notices on the road are interesting. LIFE IS SHORT DON'T MAKE IT SHORTER/THIS IS A HIGHWAY NOT A RUNWAY SO DON'T TAKE OFF. I cannot understand why, apart from lethal speed breakers on the main road, they also have them on the tracks where the surface is such that speeds of over 3 mph are impossible.

The first service I took part in was a Thanksgiving for Esther's (Benj's eldest) healing miracle. She was diagnosed with a growth between large and small intestine needing surgery. Their church and others prayed and when she returned for more tests they found the growth gone completely so no operation needed. This was wonderful for her and them as they had no money for the op. At least rents are manageable here for some folk, Rs 2,000pm for 3 rooms. They both have some land but no money to build.

I took everyone out for a meal in a hotel, 11 people, full meal cost 17 pounds total – so I shall, if alive, go to Shillong for my 90th birthday, plenty of accommodation, you are all invited but will have to pay your own fare!!!

LATER 30/11/04

I saw snow mountains from the taxi on the way on 29th. The plane was 1 hour late but there was no one to meet me in Kol. I waited an hour and then took a prepaid taxi, climbed 4 flights of stairs with all my luggage and a lot of prayer for extra strength! The flat was padlocked so I deposited the rucksacks and sat on the stairs. Kimi, a Hindu girl I met 8 years ago, appeared on the stairs above and invited me up. So we took the luggage up 2 more flights and I was given tea, home-made cakes and a sofa to rest on. Wai and Rose arrived after an hour with apologies, as Wai has met so many planes recently he thought I was on the 2 p.m. one. So now I feel at home again, sleeping on a camp bed and wandering the

streets nostalgically. Also, seeing all I left
behind here on Oct. 17th and arriving with a
full rucksack yesterday, I cannot imagine how
I got it all in! So I am sending winter clothes
and presents home by post.

6/12/04

Bez and Mike will appreciate my walk to the
central PO on the other side of Dalhousie
Squ. yesterday to post-2 airmail parcels with
calendars and winter clothes to make less
weight and more space in my big rucksack. I
had Abraham, the Cal. Bible Col. driver to help
me, as Rose said I needed a taxi and could not
get on and off trams quick enough now. We ended
up walking both ways and it took 45 minutes in
the PO. However there are now 4 policemen to
help us across Dal. Squ. by stopping all the
traffic and letting the populace surge across
at intervals! Wai went to Chennai last Thurs
with his elder brother who needed an emergency
operation on a detached retina so won't be
home before I leave, but Abraham will take me
to Howrah station. I hit my head hard on the
air-conditioner on Rose's verandah yesterday
but ice staunched the blood and the plaster on
yesterday sorted it out and it's OK.

9/12/4 TWO WEEKS IN KOLKATA

I leave Kol. on the evening of Dec. 12th and I am not staying anywhere for the next 3 weeks for more than 3 days so I may not have time to find a cafe or to write before I get home in January, but you will all be busy with Christmas. I am praying that Rose and Wai will find a couple to train to take over their work among day care centres for poor children in this area of India. It is hard to find people who can be relied on and trusted, as even Christians can be led astray when money is involved. One day they will need to "retire", though it is hard to imagine it happening when you see how hard they work. They have no property of their own as where they are in Bowbazar is rented, and when they get the 2nd of 2 adjoining flats in Behala (further out) and move all the equipment from the place on the church compound where it is stored, that will also be an 'office' with accommodation for those in charge.

I saw Wai for only 3 days as he had to go to Chennai with his brother who needed an emergency operation on detached retina. He will be back today as his brother has other family in Chennai to look after him. The operation went well.

I have enjoyed going around Kol and riding on
the underground Metro, which is very clean and
every station has a colour TV and a weighing
machine with flashing lights! Trains are always
packed and the cost for going 3 stations is 5p!
There was another strike over petrol prices
last week (they are half those in UK which
is relatively high) and so they were playing
cricket in the street! I have met Joydeep,
one of my Bible Club leaders, who attends the
oldest Baptist church here (1821) and where
I am preaching on Sunday. His sister-in-law
needs a kidney transplant and there is no one
suitable to give one free in the family and you
have to find a donor and pay them up to one lakh
(1,250 pounds) and the operation in hospital
costs the same, as there is no NHS over here.
But his church have already donated one lakh.
Yesterday I had a call from Ratan, a young
man I met 3 years ago and have corresponded
with and he came to see me and give his news.
I spoke yesterday at an AG School Assembly
and told 520 children the story of the brown
bird who wanted to know who made the beautiful
morning. I spoke from the platform using the
book, the actions and no microphone and felt
30 years younger! My voice reached the back
row, the children made cow and storm noises and

listened and gave thanks to God, the Maker of all the world. I felt like I wanted to teach again; however, I still have 5 more places to visit and help.

India continues to lurch along in spite of the bribery and corruption and I continue to get world news (mostly bad) on one of the 40 TV channels.

Thank you so much to all who pray for me. That is what enables me to cope with all events.

Note sent to people who support William in Kakinada:

Dear Janet, I am now with William. Everything fine but this is a reply to your questions, more news when I get home. He is grateful for the money towards another motorbike and it is half the price of a second-hand one. His comments – the CD player is fine and very effective for the translation of the teaching material sent. He has completed one study and xeroxed it and one copy has already been given to a man to use in his teaching. By the way rate of exchange is now Rs 82. I got the 12,300 in rupees, as it is harder for them to change sterling, as the banks want to know if they stole it!! The 3 pastors, all untrained who work together and are accountable to each other, are William, Prasad and Prem Prasad. They minister to 3 gatherings of believers, including a lot of Hindus, one of Dalits and one of fisherfolk. I shall meet each group so will report later. They want to build a church but have not money to buy the site they have found and called Sychar (John 4:5) because there is a well. They wish to preach salvation in areas where there are no live churches. Each gathering has been going 6 years. William started them when he had finished the Soon Bible Correspondence Course. He taught the other 2 pastors from his Bible studies, so I do not know the quality or depth but Jesus used fishermen, so who are we to criticise, especially as God is using all sorts in these last days? (And always has of course.) The CDs are a help both in evangelising and discipling. Books from Bangalore are useful but linkage not feasible as the distance is too great and there is no spare money. I forgot to ask re what salaries they got, if any, but will find out. I am in an Internet cafe and working at speed as it is very difficult to get Hotmail in India. So it's a three-man band and GOD. Happy Christmas. Love, Dot.

TO KAKINADA AND CHENNAI, 12-17TH DEC.

(By the way Park Street in Kolkata has been renamed Mother Teresa Sarani.)

Crossing Howrah Bridge was a change from 1988 when we missed the train because of traffic jam and people jam, as the bridge was almost empty, I have had very pleasant train journeys. William and Mary greeted me 19 hours later on the first one with 2 bunches of flowers and carried my entire luggage to the taxi. I was made welcome by rest of family and given the best bedroom, while the 5 of them piled into the other. Their son Naveen's English is better than his father's as he is at college and Mary understands my Hindi better than English. As they have 2 motorbikes I persuaded them that we should use them to go to their meetings instead of the expense of taxis and rickshaws. I really enjoyed sitting on the back of one again and it reminded me of when I went on the back of Richard's. As usual in India nothing was made very clear about when I was speaking and who to, but it worked out all right both with children and adults and lots of folk asked for prayer. Most of the women work in the paddy fields and children who have morning school help them in the afternoon. It was also good to be back in the fishing village where I opened a Bible Club 6 years ago and William would like to build a church there (but no money). As he is not a good organiser I gave some advice. There is a lot of potential here.

Velamarthi, one of my Bible Club leaders travelled through A.P. with his pastor friend and spent a morning with me, very enjoyable. William brought some black crabs home one day and they crawled over the verandah and I was taught how to eat them (when cooked) by squashing the shells, picking out the meat and sucking the legs!

The last afternoon we had a two-and-a-half-hour taxi ride to a meeting in William's home town on the delta which involved crossing the river in a barge about to fall to bits. All the meetings are in the open air using electricity from the pylons (with permission) and start late. By the time we had finished and all was cleared up it was nearly midnight and we had to be up at 04:00 to get a taxi to the station where I caught the train to Chennai. I had a deep conversation with a Brahmin Hindu who helped me off the train and a Guru type took my photograph with a mobile phone camera (cost Rs 25,000 - where would he get that sort of money?). The taxi driver at Chennai came to meet me on the platform and escort me to car (did not offer to carry my rucksack but strength was given) and we were soon in the comfort of Rachel's flat.

OFF TO PONDICHERRY 18-20TH DEC.

Mani who runs the Day Care Centre for 31 poor children down south was due to pick me up at 2 p.m. but arrived at 3 having got lost and we spent another one and a half hours trying to get out of Chennai. Then we were on National Highway 45, a 2-lane dual carriageway with a wonderful surface that should be the envy of the rest of India. We had a very fast drive in spite of the fact that some lorries go in nearside lane and others in offside, and some come in the opposite direction because they want to go somewhere where there is no access road for miles. Plus pedal bikes, carts and cows (the cows are called "brake testers"). We had an excellent driver, probably the reason he is still alive!

Pondicherry used to be a French settlement and did not join India till 1954 and it's still called Union Territory. We arrived half an hour before the children were due to go home so were able to listen to the programme they had prepared for me (songs and drama). They are boys and girls aged 4-13 and have somewhere to do homework, have a nourishing meal, and Bible teaching and love. I had the guest room (with toilet) on 2nd floor and ate with the family, Mani (ex-Indian Air Force), Joy and their 2 children. They searched a long time before they found a suitable place to rent & this is ideal. The children are well taught and local people are tutors, cooks etc. Anand is a very bright 13-year-old but I had to explain to him that in the UK people with Christian parents are often not Christians, for in India you have to be in a statistical grouping. Asher his sister of 11 looked after me very well. My Sunday "programme" started at 0815 and went on till 2200, and involved church, a tour of Pondicherry with crashing waves, French architecture plus a Sunday market thronging the centre, mango ice cream for 5 for only 60p and a final supper of Dosai, one of which was the length of the table. While the children rehearsed for the carol service, Mani and I visited one of the families who live in a bamboo hut in the slum area where 10 out of the 11 families worship the snake goddess who has her statue under a peepul tree. Cobras or vipers have visited all 10 and some have been bitten. But this 11th hut where there is a Christian family prayed for protection and have been safe. All 5 sleep in a space of 6 ft by 6 ft. The government gives each hut one electric plug so at least they have a fan. Later, I spoke to some of the parents of the children at a service on the balcony on the top floor. They are mainly Hindu but most want prayer, particularly for husbands who often have a drink problem. I got back to Chennai next morning in just over 3 hours, as we did not lose our way!

PART 3 BACK TO CHENNAI 20-23 DEC.

I have just downloaded an email from Dec 15th saying Isaac who was to meet me here tomorrow had to come home from Germany with severe hernia pain and is I know not where. However, Sebastin has phoned and will escort me south! In case you wonder who Rachel is, her husband was an Anglo-Indian & wanted to return from UK and help the poor and enable the children to go to school and college if clever. He died 6 years ago but she continues to come 4 months a year and her friend another 4 and in the hottest season they have an efficient staff. Tom said,

"It may only last 5 years", but it is now 18 years later and going well. Fortunately Tamil Nadu has a law saying that children must be educated in their native language and as Anglo Indians have English they can get into English medium schools for far less than Indians. I think I have said that most Govt schools are useless. There can only be 50 in a class, but if you have 97 you have to wait for 3 more before another teacher is appointed – hence the need for private tuition in which a lot of students are able to make some money. They are called Vine Ministries and provide food, medical expenses, school uniform, school and college fees etc as needed. Dunlop closed down recently which made a lot of unemployment. Some of the folk I have seen are so thin. Everything needs money here, as you know. Very little in our terms but a lot for them. Pray they may have wisdom to know the genuine cases. One family was living on a flyover but now have a small house. (I can imagine living UNDER a flyover but not ON one!) The birth rate does not decline, although women can have the op but usually they are not well enough after the birth and by the time they are, they are pregnant again.

They tried vasectomies for men but the men were not happy about that!!!

Yesterday I spoke to the children at the carol service in Rachel's sitting room. 52 people came and there was a teenage group playing and some solos by a girl from the UK helping in the nursery school of 180 children. Shall now return for a very late lunch and pack yet again. You will all have a wonderful Christmas I am sure and so shall I, whatever I happen to be doing.

I have just written JESUS LOVES YOU in TAMIL on the back of 70 Christmas cards cut up for the children in DKSHA.

South from Chennai Dec 23-Jan 2

I had a lovely Christmas at DKSHA. I met Isaac in Chennai on the 23rd. As I said, he had returned early from Germany with hernia pains but is managing OK. On the five-and-a half-hour train journey, 2nd-class and very fast, I was sick twice but sitting by the window so it was OK. I have been sick on and off ever since, had a fever every night, not wanting to eat at all and occasionally a bad tummy. A doctor said I might have had flu. Anyway one survives when one is asked to take meetings, and people have been looking forward to seeing you for months! The jeep ride to my old room at DKSHA was fast and I fell into bed. On Christmas Eve I managed the jeep ride to 2 Dalit villages to talk to the children, hand out cards and give them cake. Returned to bed but knew I had to manage Christmas Day. Had a bath and was sick again! Sat in the sun and talked to a gypsy headsman converted from Hinduism who was glad to hear there were lots of Christian gypsies in the UK. At 9am amidst the goats and chickens, a pile of chairs, saucepans, wood and sound boxes arrived on a 3-wheeler. I spoke to a crowded meeting of adults and children. It was a good programme with talks and dances and songs and the giving out of yellow scarves to anyone important. I gave out rest of cards and sweets to 85 children, having been told there would be 75 but there was enough for all. The 200 people then settled down for lunch and I went back to bed. Was informed we leave next day by car to Tuticorin as train took 12 hours and car only 6. However, the day went on till 22 hours.

Problems arose with Grace Ministries because of crossed wires and lack of communication. I thought I was just talking at the Prayer Conference but they wanted me to do 4 gospel meetings and children's talks as well. "They are so looking forward to your visit." I got very tired being transported vast distances in the dark along potholed country roads, deteriorating all the while. At least I had a lovely room for 3 nights in an exciseman's flat with marble floors. I felt the Lord saying, "I know these days will be difficult but it's not all bad." Woken at 04:00 by singing Hindus and at 05:00 by Muslim call to prayer – quiet after 06:00. Went upstairs to note the waterproof roofs made of interlaced coconut leaves and the milk being delivered from the churn. Did not discover there had been a tsunami early morning previous day till 12 noon. We could not go to the beach because more were expected. Growing numbers of drowned and missing reported and I was able to see BBC World News.

All the conference talks and gospel meetings went well but with sickness, sweating and lack of food I was getting worn out. I was swatting a large, malicious mosquito when I slipped on the marble floor, bashing my head and right arm. There was no one around so I got water and towels, mopped up the blood, put cold compress on arm and sat holding on bandage. Eventually someone appeared for next meeting and I was taken to a Christian doctor who washed and bandaged wounds and gave me antibiotics etc. I asked how much? His reply: "Nothing, you brought us the Gospel." Christians here are very upset about the secular humanism in the UK.

Off on Wed by 07:30 to next conference session

and then put on train to Bangalore. Ticket had not been booked on time so it was 2nd-class with no bedding supplied and I shivered all night. However, I asked for strength and was able to stagger, with my luggage, to the auto rickshaws and the luxury of Michael & Dr. Doris's home. The next 24 hours are a blank. By Fri am I was regaining normality complete with a black eye and a black arm, which has now got cellulitis so I had to go to local hospital to have intravenous injections for possible infection and a blood test to see if my blood was OK. They will email that to UK.

Off to Mumbai early Mon morning and due Heathrow at 11:30 Tuesday.

Later Michael met me and I was soon in Birmingham and on Jan. 5th was admitted to Heartlands Hospital and after a few days' wait was able to have 2 operations on the infected arm to clean it up. I had 2 weeks of very strong antibiotics and went back with Sue to be nursed back to health, for 10 days and on Jan. 24th went home and had wound dressed by district nurse until it healed. I praised the Lord for so much help from the family and the hospital and for all the prayers and for the Lord's healing. It was wonderful to be able to spend two and a half months in India.

I had a minor stroke in 2005 and was confused about a lot of things. However, when I was in hospital I apparently was writing copiously in several languages: Hindi, German, Romanian and Norwegian, all languages I had learnt a little of for my trips over the years. The doctors were fascinated and when I had recovered fully, which I thank the Lord for, I was asked to help the Stroke Society with some research!

2011

I had wanted to return to India to say goodbye to all the charities I had supported and give them more funding, but as I was less mobile now, Michael offered to take me which was a real treat.

SUMMARY OF INDIA
<u>2011</u>

THE MOST WONDERFUL HOLIDAY

DKSHA Charity, Tamil Nadu

Sunday Nov. 6. After the horrific crash on the M5 2 days earlier, Mike took the cross-country route on Saturday. We set off with the maximum

amount of luggage as I had so many gifts for the
children we would meet. The plane to Dubai was
full and there were about 10 other wheelchaired
people. We had 400 passengers and they were being
transferred to 33 different places from Dubai!!
We were transferred to the Hyderabad plane after
more wheelchair and bus rides and arrived there
next morning in lovely weather and were able to
change our money to rupees, now £1 is Rs 73 so
we were dealing with R1,000 notes!!

Orissa State kids helped by Asher Kovan

We were met at Visakhapatnam by Dr. Ravi
and driver Dayalu and set off on the 4-hour
drive to Asha Kiran. We were already late and
arrived as it got dark. As I had been twice

before I remembered the way but there had been improvements in parts of the bumpy road (in fact there is a lot of new road building going on). All the ground is now covered with plants and trees after Dr. VP, who started the work there 20 years ago, took my advice and went to a kibbutz in Israel and had their help. This place is an Indian mission for the tribal people with a hospital, schools, village outreach, care for the homeless etc.

We had an active 3 days meeting old and new friends and visiting the neighbourhood. I took the photos with me from the '90s and Dr. Ravi copied them so the changes could be seen. We had good accommodation on the 1st floor of what had originally been part of the hospital so I started continuous hands and knees up and down climbs, as there are rarely lifts in India.

We had to leave early afternoon as our next plane left at 8am. So we arrived in Visag. in the rush hour which was interesting as everyone seemed to know which bit of road to travel on whether it be the left, right, or centre and however much it altered. We eventually reached the hotel safely.

William, whom I had stayed with several times, said he would get to the hotel to see me at 8pm and subsequently arrived at 10pm as the car he borrowed had broken down, and came to our bedrooms with wife, 2 sons, and one wife and baby, plus bunches of flowers and garlands they had made and sweets for our family. They left just before midnight, having booked a nearby hotel, and the sweeper came and cleared our room of petals!

Our morning plane was cancelled and Mike arranged for us to catch another, but this was late arriving in Chennai so we missed the connection and spent the day in the Air India lounge eating, reading, resting. So it was dark when we got to Trichy but transport was awaiting with Joshua, who had been told by Isaac, who was away getting money for their work of caring for 33 homeless children, that he was to look after us. He already came regularly to help so was happy to do so and was extremely efficient. We had a less hazardous journey to DHSHA along dual carriageways, although you are allowed to go on the wrong side if you are turning right soon, but the oncoming cars just get out of the way. The girls all stayed up to 9.30pm to meet us and one had been there last time I came in 2004.

I did not recognise any of the buildings as they had all been donated since I was there. This again is an Indian-run mission.

Hooting trains and gear-changing lorries kept Mike awake all night but he departed in the morning in an air-conditioned car with Anil, his driver, to 2 days at a bird sanctuary. It was the India Children's Day that weekend and I was chief guest and spoke at the meeting for all surrounding villages in their big hall where the children danced, sang and acted. I climbed to the 3rd floor where Isabel, Isaac's wife and son lived, and walked up the hill to my abode, had cold showers and told stories to the children.

Now it was time to leave for the "holiday" part of the trip. I had never been to this part of India so I enjoyed it a lot and got a rest as well, many thanks to Mike.

Everyone waved goodbye. I know it will be my last visit but it is such a blessing to have been and I have acquired more people to write to and pray for. We had a 6-hour ride to the Nilgiri Hills along very dusty roads as they do not renew them in continuous bits but small lengths, so you have alternate smooths and bumps, but it may all get done one day. It was an impressive switch backroad to Coonoor and a luxurious stay at The Tryst, with Doc and Ann looking after us and great comfort. My friend, Daniel, originally from the north, came to stay the night. He is going back to live in Jaigaon near Bhutan, where his family live, as he finds Bangalore too commercial, in

spite of more money. Leaving there we had a
10-hour train journey to Trivandrum in Kerala
and a lovely stay at Mollys Retreat which has
a swimming pool. Michael went in the sea and
watched the fishing. We shopped and packed less
than we came with and had a peaceful journey
home by 6pm Nov. 23rd. WOW.

My life slowed down gradually over the next few
years but I was still able to pray and support
family, friends, overseas groups, and support
my church. Life continued with my family and
now seven great-grandchildren who brought
another wonderful dimension to my life.
   My life was devoted to God, peace, love and
joy.
   THE LORD BLESS YOU AND KEEP YOU
   THE LORD MAKE HIS FACE SHINE ON YOU AND
   BE GRACIOUS TO YOU
   THE LORD TURN HIS FACE TOWARDS YOU AND
   GIVE YOU PEACE

Dorothy Ada Berry 1925-2017

91st Party